SUPPER WON'T TAKE LONG

Lindsey Bareham made her name as a restaurant critic and food writer. Twenty years of reviewing the best and many of the worst restaurants provide her with a unique background for cookery writing. She writes a daily recipe for the *Evening Standard* and is food adviser to *Pie in the Sky*, the BBC series starring Richard Griffiths as chef-detective Henry Crabbe.

She is author of *The Little Book of Big Soups; A Celebration of Soup* (Penguin, 1994), shortlisted for the 1993 André Simon Award; *Sainsbury's Good Soup Book; In Praise of the Potato* (Penguin, 1995); and *Onions Without Tears* (Penguin, 1996). With Simon Hopkinson, she has co-written *Roast Chicken and Other Stories*, which won the 1994 André Simon Award and the 1995 Glenfiddich Award for Food Book of the Year, and *The Prawn Cocktail Years* (1997). She is currently writing an exhaustive tome on tomatoes.

Supper Won't Take Long

Favourite Recipes from the *Evening Standard*

LINDSEY BAREHAM

PENGUIN BOOKS

PENGUIN BOOKS

Published by the Penguin Group
Penguin Books Ltd, 27 Wrights Lane, London w8 5tz, England
Penguin Putnam Inc., 375 Hudson Street, New York, New York 10014, USA
Penguin Books Australia Ltd, Ringwood, Victoria, Australia
Penguin Books Canada Ltd, 10 Alcorn Avenue, Toronto, Ontario, Canada m4v 3b2
Penguin Books (NZ) Ltd, 182–190 Wairau Road, Auckland 10, New Zealand

Penguin Books Ltd, Registered Offices: Harmondsworth, Middlesex, England

Published in Penguin Books 1997
10 9 8 7 6 5 4 3

Set in 10.25/14 pt PostScript Monotype Baskerville
Typeset by Rowland Phototypesetting Ltd, Bury St Edmunds, Suffolk
Printed in England by Clays Ltd, St Ives plc

Contents

Suppers Without Meat 76

Dishes for One or Two 108

Suppers for Four and More 146

Puddings 200

Introduction

This is a cookery book for people who love good food but haven't always got time to spend hours shopping, chopping and cooking and who don't want to live on convenience food. That's not to say it's a book exclusively for foodies – the recipes you'll find here are practical and helpful and can be followed by anyone.

When the *Evening Standard* asked me to write their daily recipe column, which is where all these recipes come from, I couldn't believe my luck. Most people who read it are hoping to find a supper dish they can make quickly and easily when they get home. Ideally they hope for a recipe that won't involve shopping, but if it does, shopping that could be done on the way home or, if they bought an early edition, during a quick nip to the equivalent of Berwick Street Market in the lunch hour. That might mean a recipe that makes use of what's available from the corner shop, or from a not necessarily well-stocked all-purpose place. It certainly shouldn't always involve a Big Shop and shouldn't be geared towards a load of arcane ingredients.

Often the recipes recognize London's diverse food-shopping possibilities (produce and recipes from ethnic concentrations, such as Chinatown and Little India (Southall)), but the column also champions the specialist, such as a particularly good cheese shop, fishmonger or butcher, or an oddball like a Portuguese bakery or herb stockist, as well as drawing attention to wizard good buys at the multiples.

Many of the recipes don't contain meat. I'm typical of the new breed of quasi-vegetarians who no longer think that meat is vital to a balanced diet. I don't bang on about it or make it a cause, I just eat less of it and I'm far more conscious of the meat I'm eating. Economy and value for money are built into the recipes, but when something is worth splashing out on, then it is put into context: why, for example, it's worth the extra for organically produced food, and when a specialist olive oil will transform your cooking.

Above all, this is a book that understands the demands of a working person with a home to run who wants to eat healthily and well. Consequently, it's not ordered like other cookery books with starters, main dishes and desserts. Instead, it caters for the times when all you want is a snack, a private feast on your own, comfort grub, a mid-week treat for two or a hassle-free dish to offer friends, plus the occasional more ambitious dinner-party dish for the weekend.

Soup, Salad and Snack Suppers

These recipes fit the bill for the occasions when you don't want a proper supper. The times when you've had a slap-up lunch or rushed from work to the pub or to the cinema and all you want is something light and easy; something on toast, a simple but special salad, or a soup that can take care of itself.

Ironically, many of these dishes, such as toasted muffins slathered with cream and piled with slippery mushrooms and crisp bacon, roasted onion and tomato soup with green dumplings, and prawn tzaziki with dill and coriander, would make ideal hors d'œuvre for a posh dinner party. Others, such as wild rice salad with mushroom vinaigrette, caramelized onion, tomatoes and feta cheese, and spiced aubergine salad with sour cream and red onion, could also be served as side dishes, to vegetarians, or as part of a buffet.

Caesar Salad

Serves 4   *Preparation: 15 minutes. Cooking: 5 minutes*

6 little gem lettuce hearts

For the dressing:
1 egg yolk
175ml vegetable oil
1 tbsp red wine vinegar
2 garlic cloves, crushed to a
   paste
6 anchovy fillets, canned in
   oil, drained and chopped
juice of 1 lemon

1 heaped tbsp freshly grated
   Parmesan
1 tbsp water

For the croutons:
4 garlic cloves
6 tbsp olive oil
12 × 1½cm-thick slices slightly
   stale baguette
salt and cayenne pepper
chunk of Parmesan

Legend has it that on Independence Day in 1924, Caesar Cardini, boss of the Caesar's Palace in Tijuana, Mexico, found his cupboard bare when a gang of Hollywood greats turned up to celebrate. Being an Italian he was able to conjure out of the larder various key ingredients which inspired a salad of crisp lettuce leaves dressed with lightly cooked egg, olive oil, lemon and a hint of Worcester sauce, garnished with garlic croutons and Parmesan.

I've never come across a so-called authentic recipe for this infamous salad, although Cardini's daughter Rosa now markets the dressing.

Some people purée the anchovy into the dressing. Others include whole anchovies, usually the sort preserved in oil, scattered over the finished salad. I prefer to copy Charles Fontaine of the Chop House, chopping and mixing them in with the dressing.

The lettuce has to be cos (Romaine) or something similar like little gem. I'm ambivalent about the Parmesan. Not about using it, but how it's treated. Cardini, I'm sure, would have grated it over the dressed salad. There's a case, though, for shaving flakes of it instead, so you get concentrated chunks of flavour. Another controversial area is whether to include Worcester sauce or not. I don't. And then there's the croutons. Some people go for croûtes (usually matched with flakes of Parmesan), or croutons so hard and big they resemble dog biscuits. Whatever shape or size you prefer garlic is vital.

All in all, for a salad with so few ingredients, there's one heck of a lot of things to think about.

1. Separate the lettuce leaves and rinse in cold water. Drain, dry thoroughly and, if necessary, cut into bite-sized pieces.

2. Next make the croutons. Pre-heat the oven to 400F/200C/ gas mark 6. Crush the garlic with the flat of a knife, peel off the skin and place in a frying pan with the oil. Heat through for a couple of minutes, then turn off the heat. Cut each slice of bread into four. Scoop the garlic out of the pan and quickly toss the bread in the hot oil. Tip the croutons into a roasting tin and bake in the oven for 5 minutes until golden but not brown. Season lightly with salt and cayenne. Drain on kitchen paper.

3 Make the dressing by beating the egg yolk in a bowl, then slowly add the oil in a thin trickle, thinning every now and again with some of the vinegar, to make a thick mayonnaise. Stir in the garlic paste, chopped anchovy and lemon juice, then add the Parmesan and finally the water, a few drops at a time, until you achieve a thick and creamy consistency.

4. To serve, place the lettuce leaves in a bowl and loosely toss with the dressing – as much as you like; leftovers will keep in the fridge for a few days. Mix in the croutons and finish with plenty of cheese (grated, or flaked with a sharp potato peeler).

Chive and Potato Galettes, Celery and Anchovy Mayonnaise with Ham

Serves 4   *Preparation: 20 minutes. Cooking: 20 minutes*

500g lukewarm or cold, boiled
   new potatoes
1 plump garlic clove
1 large shallot
2 tbsp chopped chives
2 eggs
salt and freshly milled black
   pepper
1 head of celery

For the dressing:
3 tbsp Hellmann's mayonnaise

1 tbsp Dijon mustard
1 tbsp red wine vinegar
3 tbsp olive oil
5 anchovy fillets
1 tbsp chopped flat-leaf
   parsley
freshly milled black pepper
butter and oil for frying
8 or more slices prosciutto or
   other good ham

When I was nineteen and providing for myself for the first time, I lived in a huge flat off the Fulham Road. None of us could cook properly and most of our attempts at fresh food were, frankly, diabolical.

Occasionally there were breakthroughs when someone learned to make something tasty and quick that cost next to nothing and used ingredients we could obtain from a local corner shop.

One of my jackpots was the discovery that if you grated raw potato and fried it fast and furiously you ended up with a lacy pancake that needed no more than a sprinkle of salt and a squirt of tomato ketchup.

This recipe is a refinement of those pancakes. These days I use leftover cooked potatoes and flavour the pancakes with chives and diced onion.

I wish I'd thought of using cooked potatoes all those years ago because it makes the preparation far less of a hassle although you need egg – rather than the starch in raw potatoes – to hold the pancake together. I make them thin and big and fold them over a contrasting filling.

They are excellent, for example, with a dollop of cold apple purée and one of Greek yoghurt with crisply grilled bacon. Here I've matched them with finely sliced celery held in an anchovy mayonnaise.

This is good on its own, but with a few slices of decent ham it's even better.

1. Peel and finely chop the garlic and the shallot. Whisk the eggs. Season well with salt and pepper. Grate the potatoes into the eggs, add the garlic, shallot and chopped chives. Mix thoroughly.
2. Trim the celery, removing the root, but keep it in a bunch. Using a large, sharp knife, slice finely starting from the root end. Tip into a colander, rinse under cold running water and drain.
3. Place the Hellmann's in a mixing bowl. Stir in the mustard, then the vinegar and olive oil, and season generously with black pepper. Chop the anchovy fillets and add to the bowl with the parsley. Add the celery and mix.
4. Divide the potato mixture in four. Heat a frying pan very hot, add a knob of butter and a scant tablespoon of cooking oil. Swirl around the pan and add the potato, smoothing it over with the back of a spoon to cover the pan entirely. Cook at a moderate heat for 4 minutes, flip over – it sets quite firm – and repeat. Slip on to a plate, spoon on a share of the celery, top with ham and fold over the pancake. Eat immediately.

Compote of Summer Vegetables with Watercress

Serves 2–4   *Preparation: 15 minutes. Cooking: 15 minutes*

900ml light chicken stock	6 runner beans
½ tsp salt	225g shelled peas
bunch of spring onions	2 plum tomatoes
8 (or more) tiny new potatoes	2 egg yolks
1 medium carrot	juice of 1 lemon
1 courgette	1 big bunch watercress

In June and July, when the greengrocers' shelves are piled high with the best of British vegetables and salad stuff, it's daft not to make the most of it. This soup is made with a mixture of some of these young vegetables, cooked in stock until just tender.

The combination and quantities I've chosen are not written in stone, merely what were available to me on the day I made up the recipe. It would be just as good made with, say, cauliflower or broccoli florets, whole spring onions, asparagus tips and sweetcorn. You could even add scraps of lean chicken at the beginning of cooking to make more of a meal of it.

The soup is finished off with a liaison of egg yolks and lemon juice in the style of avgolemono, the ubiquitous Greek soup. This has the dual purpose of thickening and enriching while injecting a pleasingly fresh yet creamy flavour.

Finely chopped watercress, stirred in just before serving, adds a sharp peppery tang to this lovely soup. If watercress isn't available, and you do need plenty of it, a similar result comes from using rocket. The soup is also good, but without the pungent kick, finished with finely shredded young spinach or lettuce, or with masses of finely chopped soft green herbs.

The quantities given are sufficient for a light supper for two – perhaps with bread and cheese and a substantial pud to follow – or a hors d'œuvre for four.

1. Bring the stock to a gentle, steady simmer with the salt.

2. Meanwhile prepare all the vegetables and keep them in separate piles. Scrape the potatoes and rinse. Trim the spring onions and slice the white and tender green parts into chunky pieces. Peel the carrot, quarter lengthways and chop into dice. Top and tail the runner beans and slice thinly on the slant in the old-fashioned style. Trim the courgette, quarter lengthways and dice. Place the tomatoes in a bowl and cover with boiling water. Count to twenty, drain and refresh under cold running water. Peel away the skin, quarter the tomatoes and remove seeds and core. Slice each quarter into three strips and chop into dice. Remove all the leaves from the watercress and chop finely – you want to end up with at least 5 tablespoons, preferably more.

3. Whisk the egg yolks and lemon juice together.

4. Add the potatoes to the simmering stock and cook for 5 minutes. Add the spring onions to the pan and, when the simmer is re-established, cook for 30 seconds and then add the carrots. When the stock is simmering happily again, cook for 1 minute and add the peas. Wait for a return to simmer, count 30 seconds and add the beans. Repeat and add the courgettes, followed by the tomatoes. Re-establish simmer and cook for 30 seconds. Turn the heat very low.

5. Scoop a ladleful of soup and stir it into the egg yolk and lemon juice mixture. Pour it back into the soup, stirring as you pour, and simmer very gently for 1 minute, taking care not to let it boil. Stir in the watercress and serve immediately.

Fattoush

Serves 4–6   *Preparation: 30 minutes. Cooking: 2 minutes*

1 medium cucumber
4 large shallots, 2 banana
    shallots, bunch of spring
    onions or 2 medium red
    onions
500g tomatoes
1 celery heart (at least 4 sticks
    with fronds)
1 slice pitta bread
½ tbsp salt

1 very large bunch of flat-leaf
    parsley
1 tbsp roughly chopped mint
3 tbsp roughly chopped
    coriander
2 plump garlic cloves
juice of 1 lemon
6 tbsp olive oil
salt and freshly milled black
    pepper

To get maximum pleasure from making this salad you will need two sharp knives – one small triangular turning or paring knife and a larger broad-pointed cook's knife. This is most definitely a salad that is all about chopping and slicing, and it will be misery to attempt with a blunt knife.

It is a wonderful mixture of fresh, slightly acidic flavours with a kickback of garlic and a nuttiness that comes from the salad's 'garnish' of toasted pitta bread.

Fattoush is a Middle Eastern salad which pops up on many Lebanese menus, but it was while leafing through Paula Wolfert's recently republished *Mediterranean Cooking* that it caught my eye again. To be really authentic, as in the recipe in this excellent book, you will need to hunt out a blend of Middle Eastern herbs called za'atar, which features a tart, red spice called sumac.

As I happened to have a supply of the Moroccan spice mix, ras el hanout, I added a little of that to my version of fattoush but I'm not convinced that any of these extra sharp, resinous flavours are essential. What is essential is some decent tomatoes with flavour, a nice firm cucumber, a huge bunch of flat-leaf parsley and smaller bunches of coriander and mint.

Extra crunch could come from a sweet red pepper or, as in my recipe, celery. The best onion to use would be a few of those pink-grey shallots from France, but failing that, spring onions or red onions would be preferable to a bog standard brown onion.

1. Use a potato peeler to peel the cucumber, split lengthways and use a teaspoon to gouge out the seeds. Cut into lengths and dice the flesh. Tip into a colander, dredge with ½ tablespoon of salt and leave to drain while you do all the rest of the chopping.
2. Peel and finely dice the onion. Place the tomatoes in a bowl, cover with boiling water, count to twenty, drain. Quarter the tomatoes, remove their seeds and skin, then dice the flesh. Trim then very finely slice the celery, tip into a colander and rinse thoroughly under cold running water. Drain carefully.
3. Split the pitta bread in half and toast both sides until crisp. When cool enough to handle, crumble into small pieces.
4. Pick all the leaves off the parsley stalks and chop very finely.
5. Peel the garlic, chop roughly then sprinkle with a scant half-teaspoon of salt and pulverize with the flat of a blade to make a creamy paste. Tip the garlic paste into a salad bowl, stir in the lemon juice and whisk in the olive oil. Tip in the onions, then the celery, then the tomatoes and herbs, stirring as you make each addition.

Tip the cucumber into a clean tea towel and wring it dry. Add to the dish and season generously with black pepper. Give one final toss and strew the pitta bread over the top. Fold in the bread 5 minutes before you eat.

Herb Soup with Chervil Cream and Wholemeal Sage Scones

Serves 4   *Preparation: 30 minutes. Cooking: 40 minutes*

For the scones:
250g self-raising wholemeal
    flour
½ tsp salt
125g butter or hard margarine
1 tbsp finely chopped fresh
    sage
150ml milk
1 egg whisked with 1 tbsp milk
    or 1 tbsp flour

For the soup:
25g butter
6 spring onions
500g new potatoes

900ml light chicken stock (or
    equivalent made with
    stock cubes)
6 tbsp finely chopped mixed
    fresh herbs such as
    watercress, rocket, parsley,
    basil, mint, chervil and
    chives
salt and pepper

For the chervil cream:
1 tbsp roughly chopped
    chervil
4 tbsp crème fraîche
lemon juice

As a dedicated user of fresh herbs, I'm very happy to do my bit to help promote National Herb Week, which takes place each year in June. Barely a day goes by when I don't use herbs in my cooking, but this recipe was devised to use as many garden herbs as I could lay my hands on. The soup is really a summer potato soup with herbs added right at the end so they keep their colour and flavour. This recipe works well with one or a combination or any of the soft herbs listed. Rocket, for example, on its own and uncut, is wonderful with potatoes. The chervil cream, which sounds rather grander than it actually is, works particularly well with chives, parsley or basil, but a mixture of herbs is good too. The scones are a quick, foolproof recipe. I've made them with onions and Parmesan, and with rosemary as well as thyme.

1. Begin by making the scones. Pre-heat the oven to 375F/190C/ gas mark 5.

2. Tip the flour into a mixing bowl with the salt. Cut the butter or margarine into small pieces and rub it into the flour until the mixture resembles rough breadcrumbs. Stir in the sage and gradually add the milk to form a soft, pliable dough. Turn it on to a floured surface and gently pat and mould the dough to form a slab 18 × 25cm. Cut across its width into three equal pieces and divide each band into three triangles. If you have time, rest the dough for 20 minutes. Transfer to a flat, well-greased baking tray and brush the tops with the egg wash or dust with flour. Bake for 10 minutes, lower the oven temperature to 300F/150C/gas mark 2 and cook for a further 10 minutes until puffed and golden.

3. While the scones are baking, prepare the vegetables for the soup. Trim and finely slice the onions and scrape and chop the potatoes.

4. Melt the butter in a large saucepan and gently sweat the spring onions until softened. This takes about 5 minutes. Add the potatoes, pour on the stock and bring to the boil. Simmer vigorously for 15 minutes until the potatoes are tender. Purée the soup in a liquidizer, food processor or mouli-légumes and season to taste. Just before serving, stir in the mixed herbs and reheat. To make the chervil cream, mix the chervil into the crème fraîche with a tiny squeeze of lemon juice.

Serve the soup with a dollop of chervil cream.

Horse Mushroom Muffins and Bacon

Serves 2   *Preparation: 10 minutes. Cooking: 8 minutes*

200g large horse mushrooms
25g butter
1 plump garlic clove
2 tbsp freshly snipped chives
squeeze lemon juice
1 tbsp cooking oil
8 rashers thin-cut streaky
    bacon

4 English muffins
6 tbsp double or whipping
    cream
salt and freshly ground
    pepper

This recipe could be made with any mushrooms, but for a change I chose horse mushrooms.

Horse mushrooms, particularly the big ones, would look at home in a Disney cartoon and are tall yet stumpy; a bit like a puffball that hasn't puffed or a baby cep with a super-smooth cap that hugs a plump stem. There is a faint almond whiff to them and their very pale skin quickly turns golden when fried.

Like puffballs and ceps, the flesh is firm and uniformly dense and its flavour is more assertive than most other cultivated mushrooms. They could be used in any recipe that calls for mushrooms, but their relatively high price puts them in the luxury class.

For this snack, the mushrooms are thinly sliced and fried in butter with a sprinkling of garlic and chives. They are then piled on to toasted English muffins which have been spread with a thick layer of whipped cream.

This voluptuous version of mushrooms on toast makes a wonderful bite that will drive you mad with mouthwatering smells as it cooks. It is, however, smart enough to serve at a dinner party. The chewy texture of the muffins (which, incidentally, quickly drink up the cream and mushroom juices) goes very well with the slippery, buttery and faintly garlicky mushrooms.

And when a few rashers of crisp bacon are added on the side, with the whole thing smartened up with a sprinkling of chives and a final dollop of cream, it becomes sheer indulgence.

1. Rinse the mushrooms under cold running water, picking off any 'earth' that clings to the stem. Don't attempt to peel the mushrooms. Thinly slice lengthways. Peel and dice the garlic.

2. Melt the butter in a frying pan over a medium-low flame and when it's frothing, throw in the mushrooms. Toss quickly to coat with butter and cook for a couple of minutes before seasoning lightly with salt and pepper – once you've done this the juices will start to flow.

3. Immediately sprinkle over the garlic and half the chives and stir around. Leave to stew gently for a few minutes letting the juices concentrate and evaporate as the mushrooms turn tender – you may need to turn the heat up towards the end of cooking to speed this up. Taste and adjust the seasoning with salt, pepper and a squeeze of lemon.

4. Meanwhile, halve the bacon rashers and fry or grill on both sides until really crisp. Drain on absorbent kitchen paper.

5. When everything is just about ready, lightly toast the muffins and whip the cream until thick, floppy and spreadable. Thickly spread the muffins with just over half the cream, divide the mushrooms among them and sprinkle with the remaining chives. Spoon a big dollop of cream on to each muffin. Tuck the bacon alongside. Devour.

Leek and Potato Bruschetta with Chive Boursin and Tomatoes

Serves 2   *Preparation: 15 minutes. Cooking: 10 minutes*

4 leeks

4 medium new potatoes

8 small tasty tomatoes

1 tsp salt

small bunch of chives

1 plump new-season garlic
  clove

4 tbsp vinaigrette

approx. 6 tbsp fruity olive oil

125g pot Boursin en habit de
  Ciboulette

4 thick slices sourdough or
  pain de campagne

2 eggs

10 Niçoise or other decent
  black olives

salt and pepper

Real bruschetta – pronounced brussketta not brooshetta – is made with crusty country bread, toasted and rubbed with garlic while still hot, then seasoned generously with good-quality fruity olive oil and sea salt.

The best bruschetta is made on the barbecue. The bread is toasted on one side and the toasted side is scoured with garlic, then dribbled all over with olive oil before going back on the barbecue, untoasted side down.

The second-best bruschetta is made on a rib-top grill pan, which also gives it those attractive sear marks.

But however you make it, be it on the barbecue, rib-top grill, conventional grill or in the oven, bruschetta gets my vote for breathing new life into things on toast, including baked beans.

Style victims who think the word bruschetta *passé* could always call this delicious garlic toast something different. Fettunta or Panunto (Tuscan and Lazio region alternatives) would do it.

The Boursin, incidentally, is part of a new range designed for the cheeseboard.

1. Trim the leeks and cut the white and pale-green parts on the slant into 5cm chunks. Peel the potatoes and quarter. Bring a large pan of water to the boil, add 1 teaspoon of salt and fling in the leeks. Cook at a vigorous boil until tender, checking with the point of a sharp knife after 4 minutes. Drain. Meanwhile, place the potatoes in a separate saucepan, cover generously with water, add salt and boil until tender. When the potato water is boiling, add the eggs to the pan and cook (from boiling) for 5 minutes. The potatoes should also be ready. Drain. Crack the egg shell all over, hold under running cold water and peel immediately.

2. While all that's cooking, prepare everything else. Cut the tomatoes into quarters. Use scissors or a very sharp knife to snip the chives finely. Peel the garlic and halve.

3. Pour the vinaigrette into a suitable bowl, stir in the leeks, tossing them thoroughly to coat evenly before adding the potatoes, then the tomatoes and half the chives. Season generously with salt and pepper.

4. Toast the bread. If using a toaster or overhead grill, toast the bread and then rub one side with garlic and dribble generously with olive oil. If using a hob-top ridged grill pan, smear both sides of the bread with olive oil first and cook it on the preheated, un-oiled grill pan. Rub the toast with garlic on one side. Spread the garlic-rubbed toast thickly with Boursin and pile the leek mixture over the toasts. Sprinkle on the remaining chives, add some of the black olives and place the egg on the side.

Prawn Tzaziki with Dill and Coriander

Serves 4 as a starter, 2 for supper

Preparation: 30 minutes.
Cooking: 30 minutes

200g raw tiger prawns with
shells
1 garlic clove
1 medium onion
1 stick of celery
1 carrot
1 tomato
1 bay leaf
pinch of salt, 4 black
peppercorns

600ml water
300ml Greek yoghurt
½ cucumber
4 drops Tabasco
1 small garlic clove
2 tbsp chopped mint
1 tbsp chopped dill fronds
1 tbsp coriander leaves
salt and freshly milled black
pepper

This is a lovely light summery dish which would make an elegant starter or could be turned into a satisfying supper. It's made by poaching raw tiger prawns and mixing them into thick Greek yoghurt, seasoned with some of the poaching broth.

The dish earns the name tzaziki because it's modelled on the Greek cucumber, mint and yoghurt dip-cum-salad.

Served as a starter it goes well with a simple tomato salad glazed with a sweet vinaigrette and thin slices of buttered brown bread on the side. As a supper dish it works well with a crisp green salad made with little gem, and a big bowl of mixed green vegetables such as peas, runner beans and courgettes, cooked al dente.

The resultant prawn stock will be packed with flavour – prawn shells make excellent stock – and is worth saving and stashing away in the freezer. It would be the perfect base for a Mediterranean fish soup. In fact, all you need to do is sauté one finely chopped onion, two crushed garlic cloves and one finely sliced fennel bulb in 2 tablespoons of olive oil for 10 minutes before adding four peeled and chopped medium tomatoes and a 5cm piece of orange zest. Simmer for 5 minutes before adding the prawn stock, a pinch of saffron, salt and pepper, and cook for another 5 minutes before adding 500g of white fish cut into bite-sized chunks. Once the fish is firm and white it's ready.

1. Tip the prawns out of their bag, spreading them out so they defrost quickly. Meanwhile, crack the first garlic clove with your fist and flake off its skin. Peel and dice the onion and finely chop the celery, carrot and tomato. Place the garlic, onion, celery, carrot, tomato, bay leaf, a pinch of salt and 4 peppercorns in a pan with 600ml water. Bring to the boil and simmer gently. By now the prawns should be sufficiently defrosted to peel off their shells. Add them to the stock pot. Simmer gently for 20 minutes, then strain and reserve the stock, pouring it back in the pan. Bring back to simmer, add the prawns and watch as their colour changes to mottled pink; this takes about 1 minute. Turn off the heat, cover the pan and leave for 5 minutes. Drain, reserving the stock, and spread the prawns out on a plate to cool.

2. Peel the second garlic clove and pulverize it with a little salt. Place the yoghurt in a serving bowl. Stir in the garlic and 3 tablespoons of the reserved stock, then 4 drops of Tabasco, mixing thoroughly before adding the mint, dill and half the coriander. Taste and season with pepper. Chop the prawns in half and add to the bowl. Peel the cucumber, slice it very thinly and mix it in with everything else. Sprinkle over the rest of the coriander and serve.

Roasted Onion and Tomato Soup with Green Dumplings

Serves 4–6   *Preparation: 10 minutes. Cooking: 45 minutes*

3 Spanish onions

900g plum tomatoes

4 big garlic cloves

2 medium carrots

1 chicken stock cube dissolved
    in 300ml boiling water

salt and freshly milled black
    pepper

For the dumplings:

100g soft goats cheese

50g fresh breadcrumbs

1 tbsp each of finely chopped
    chives, parsley, mint and
    basil or fresh coriander

1 large egg

This is one of those dream soups that's as easy and undemanding to make as it's impressive to look at. It goes without saying that it tastes good too.

You don't have to get involved with chopping and fiddling around with this soup; tomatoes, onions, garlic and carrot are bunged in the oven to soften and concentrate their flavours. Then they're liquidized and used as a poaching broth for light, dainty little dumplings.

If the idea of cooking dumplings rings alarm bells, don't let it put you off making this recipe. They really are child's play and turn a good soup into something special.

I drove my publishers mad when I was writing *A Celebration of Soup* (Penguin) because I became obsessed with things that can be added to or served with soup. This is the fun side of soup-making, when you can get artistic and give bog-standard soups your personal stamp. This soup, for example, would also be good garnished with a spoonful of chopped fresh tomato, perhaps mixed with coriander or basil. Or how about serving it with a dollop of pesto or a fresh herb cream, or lightly cooked diced courgettes and peas stirred in at the last minute?

1. Turn the oven to 400F/200C/gas mark 6.

2. Halve the onions through their middles, trim away the roots but leave the skins on. Crack the garlic with a clenched fist. Trim the carrots and split them lengthways into quarters.

3. Place the onion halves cut side down on a heavy baking tray. Stand the tomatoes on their core end and tuck the garlic and carrots around them. Bake for 40 minutes.

4. Meanwhile make the dumplings. Put the goats cheese in a bowl and mash it well with a fork. Mix in the breadcrumbs and herbs and season with salt and pepper. Beat the egg and mix it into the cheese mixture. Take a teaspoon of the mixture and, with a second teaspoon, mould it into a little dumpling. Continue until all the mixture is used up.

5. When the vegetables are cooked, whip off their skins and tip the whole lot, juices and all, into the bowl of a food processor. Liquidize and pour the soup through a sieve into a saucepan. Add the stock. Heat until simmering, adjust the seasoning with salt and pepper and add the dumplings. Poach for 3–4 minutes until firm. Serve immediately.

Scallops with Leeks, Mash and Pancetta

Serves 4　　　　　　　　*Preparation: 30 minutes. Cooking: 20 minutes*

3 medium to large potatoes
50g butter
2 tbsp thick cream
3 tbsp milk
3 large scallops, approx. 250g
　in total
1 glass white wine
1 bay leaf
1 small onion, chopped

2 long pale leeks
3 slices pancetta
2 tbsp chopped parsley
2 tbsp white breadcrumbs
1 tbsp freshly grated
　Parmesan
salt and freshly milled black
　pepper

Scallop shells make an attractive receptacle for this dish, but you can make individual servings – it's that sort of dish – in small gratin dishes.

The scallops and their vast bright-orange corals are separated before being poached in seasoned white wine.

They are then diced and mixed with chopped pancetta and quite a lot of parsley, and held in a thick leek sauce made by puréeing cooked leek with a little cream and some of the reduced poaching liquid.

This tasty combination is surrounded by stiff mashed potato, made with just enough milk, butter and cream to make it rich and malleable, but strong enough to serve as a wall to hold the mixture. The top is covered with breadcrumbs mixed with grated Parmesan.

All this can be done in advance and it then needs about 20

minutes in the oven to finish off the cooking and give the potato some crusty edges.

1. Peel the potatoes, cut into even-sized pieces and cook in plenty of salted water. Drain and dry mash, by either passing through a mouli-légumes or pressing through a sieve with the back of a wooden spoon. Beat in 25g of the butter, 3 tablespoons of milk and 1 tablespoon thick cream.

2. Meanwhile, rinse the scallops, trimming away any suspect pieces including the tough bit of muscle where it was attached to the shell. Remove the corals. Boil the wine, bay leaf and onion in a small saucepan. Reduce the heat immediately and simmer for 5 minutes before adding the scallops. Simmer gently for a couple of minutes.

3. Remove the scallops and set aside to cool. Slice the coral into chunks and cut the white meat into similar-sized pieces.

4. Meanwhile, finely chop and rinse the leeks. Soften the remaining butter in a small pan, add the leeks, seasoning with salt and pepper, cover the pan and cook over a moderate heat for about 6 minutes until soft but uncoloured. Remove the lid, increase the heat, boiling for a minute or two to get rid of any liquid.

5. Tip the leeks into the bowl of a food processor and blitz with 1 tablespoon of the thick cream and 2 tablespoons of the wine to make a thickish sauce.

Chop the pancetta and mix it, along with the parsley and scallops, into the purée. Spoon into shells or small gratin dishes. Surround with spoonfuls of mash, forking it up to form a wall. Dust the entire surface with the cheese mixed with the breadcrumbs. Cook in the oven at 375F/190C/gas mark 5 for 20 minutes until burnished and bubbling.

Spiced Aubergine Salad with Sour Cream and Red Onion

Serves 6   *Preparation: 30 minutes.*
Cooking: 45–60 minutes, plus 1 hour (or more) to chill

3 medium aubergines
1 tbsp salt
100ml olive oil
2 Spanish onions
8 plum tomatoes
3 garlic cloves
1 heaped tsp ground cumin
1 heaped tsp ground allspice
¼ tsp cayenne pepper
2 heaped tbsp currants
2 heaped tbsp chopped fresh
    mint

2 heaped tbsp chopped fresh
    coriander
salt
1 tbsp chopped fresh mint
    stirred into 100ml
    Greek-style natural
    yoghurt
1 medium red onion
juice from ½ lemon
cayenne pepper

This is a variation on the gooey Turkish salad dish called Imam Bayeldi and is succulent and sweet yet hauntingly spicy and very moreish. It's the sort of dish that I like to make for no particular reason, to tuck into chilled from the fridge when I can't be bothered to cook. I like it scooped up with toasted pitta bread with creamy yoghurt on the side, or with a slab of glistening feta cheese. It's almost a meal on its own and goes well with baked potatoes or with other Middle Eastern dishes such as hummus and silky-smooth moutabal, the best of all aubergine dips.

Its exact origin is unknown in a way that's often the case with popular restaurant dishes as they pass between chefs and kitchens. I first ate it at Bibendum, and then at Blueprint Café when Lucy

Crabb was chef. I've since seen it on the menu at Fifth Floor, Bluebird's Club and Bruce's Bistro in Wandsworth. The link here is that all these restaurant chefs worked in Bibendum's kitchen at the same time as Nikki Barraclough who, until recently, cooked at Arcadia. She picked it up from someone at the Carved Angel in Devon. Anyway, I do urge you to try it.

1. Chop the aubergines into 1cm cubes. Pile into a colander and sprinkle with one tablespoon of salt. Leave for 30 minutes.
2. Peel and finely chop the Spanish onions. Blanch the tomatoes in boiling water for 20 seconds. Remove the tomato skins and cores and coarsely chop the flesh. Peel and finely chop the garlic.
3. Heat half the olive oil in a spacious pan, stir in the onions and gently sauté until tender and pale golden. This will take about 20 minutes. Mix in the tomatoes, spices and garlic. Stew gently for 10 minutes, stir in the currants and turn off the heat.
4. Rinse the salt off the aubergines and pat dry with absorbent kitchen paper.
5. In a wok or your largest frying pan, heat the remaining olive oil until smoking. Tip in the aubergines and stir-fry until golden all over and cooked through. This will take about 15 minutes but you may need to do it in two batches. Mix both sets of ingredients together in a large bowl, stir in the fresh herbs and leave to cool. Taste for seasoning; you may need more salt.
6. Peel, halve and cut the red onion into wafer-thin slices. Leave to marinate for at least 15 minutes in the lemon juice. Drain.

Serve the aubergine cold with some of the mint-laced yoghurt on the side and, if liked, cover it with drained and now mildly flavoured bright pink onion slices. Dust with cayenne.

Vidalia and Anchovy Tarts

Makes 4 tarts   *Preparation: 30 minutes. Cooking: 80 minutes*

4 Vidalia or Spanish onions
  (approx. 225g each)
4 tbsp olive oil
3 sprigs fresh thyme or ½ tsp
  herbes de Provence
1 bay leaf
salt and freshly milled black
  pepper

225g defrosted ready-rolled
  puff pastry
2 tbsp tomato or sun-dried
  tomato purée
50g can anchovy fillets,
  drained and split
  lengthways

'Vidalia?' you may well ask. 'What on earth are Vidalia?'

Vidalia are onions so sweet and pale that they can be eaten like an apple and with such a high water content they're juicy beyond compare. Vidalia are new to this country, raised in Georgia and thought to be a distant relative of Spanish onions.

You'll recognize them immediately if you see them because, apart from being big like Spanish onions, they have flaky, soft, pale skins and all carry a batch number, in much the same way as some apples do.

Vidalia are a joy to cook with because they really don't make you cry and are wonderful treated as a vegetable in their own right.

Try them, for example, peeled and trimmed (so they sit flat) and baked in the oven with a pat of butter or a splash of olive oil, and a seasoning of salt and pepper, for around 45 minutes at 350F/180C/gas mark 4.

I've used Vidalia – pronounced vy-dale-yuh – in this variation on pissaladière, the onion and anchovy tart that's a speciality of

Nice and is sold in square slabs wrapped in a piece of waxed paper.

Spanish onions would do just as well: what's important is that the onions are sweet and have a high water content so that they cook down.

This is smeared over pastry – in Nice it would be pizza dough – and decorated with anchovy which melts slightly into the onions.

1. Peel, halve and finely slice the onions. Heat 3 tablespoons of the olive oil in a large, lidded casserole and stir in the onions with the thyme or herbes de Provence and bay leaf. Cook for 10 minutes, stirring occasionally, then cover the pan and leave to cook gently, stirring a couple of times, for 30 minutes. Remove the lid, season generously with salt and pepper and cook for a further 30 minutes until the onions are thoroughly softened and a pale-golden-brown colour. Whip out the thyme, if using, and bay leaf.

2. Use a sharp knife to cut the pastry into four equal pieces. On a lightly floured surface roll out each piece of pastry until it measures (approximately) 15 × 15cm. Transfer the squares to a baking tray greased with the remaining olive oil, leaving a gap between them. Lightly prick the pastry with a fork so it doesn't rise up in the middle and push the onions off. Leaving a 1cm border, spread each square with some of the tomato paste.

3. Pre-heat the oven to 425F/220C/gas mark 7.

4. Place some of the onions on each piece of pastry and spread to cover the tomato purée (within 1cm of the edge). Brush the border with olive oil. Decorate each tart with a lattice of anchovies.

5. Bake in the pre-heated oven for 10–15 minutes until the border is puffed and golden and the underneath is nicely crisp.

Vietnamese Spring Rolls with Chilli Dipping Sauce

Serves 4   *Preparation: 15 minutes. Cooking: 20 minutes*

½ tsp salt
16 circular rice paper
   pancakes (banh trang)
1 small raw chicken breast or
   a handful of cooked
   shelled prawns
3 spring onions
1 carrot
50g beansprouts
½ small red pepper
2 tbsp frozen peas
25g thin rice noodles
1 tbsp roughly chopped mint
   leaves
1 tbsp roughly chopped
   coriander leaves

2 tbsp roasted and roughly
   ground peanuts
16 curls of crisp lettuce
   (optional)
extra mint and coriander
   leaves

Dipping sauce:
1 small fresh red chilli pepper
   or ½ tsp Tabasco
½ small garlic clove
½ tsp sugar
1 tbsp rice vinegar
1 tbsp Thai fish sauce
squeeze of lime juice

As a snack, next time you find yourself near an oriental food shop, preferably a Thai one, I recommend that you buy a packet of galettes de riz. These look like creamy white poppadams and often have a linoleum-style pattern etched on to their surface.

Rice-paper pancakes are extraordinary things which are stiff and brittle, but when slipped into a bowl of hot water they soften and become malleable and transparent.

This process takes a matter of seconds and, rather than prepare the spring rolls in advance, as I'm advocating in this recipe, it's a good ruse to lay out all the stuffing ingredients in piles and let people make their own. Those experienced in roll-your-own techniques will rattle through the process, but fumblers might find the assembly a bit fiddly.

You can stuff anything you like in these spring rolls, and there's no reason why they shouldn't be made with European ingredients and sweet as well as savoury things.

Because the finished result is see-through, it works well to include some contrasting colours, too – diced red pepper, whole leaves of coriander and shreds of lettuce and carrot are all good.

1. Bring a large pan of water to the boil and add the salt. Meanwhile, trim and finely shred the spring onions. Finely dice the red pepper. Peel and grate the carrot. When the water is boiling, throw the beansprouts into the pan and cook for 30 seconds.
2. Remove with a slotted spoon. Do the same with the peas and then with the rice noodles, keeping each drained pile separate. Put all the vegetable trimmings in the pan and cook the chicken at a gentle simmer for 15 minutes. Remove from the pan and shred. Halve the prawns
3. To make the dipping sauce, de-seed and finely chop the red chilli pepper. Crush, peel and finely chop the garlic and combine all remaining ingredients in a small dish.
4. To assemble the rolls, have ready a bowl with 5cm of hot water. Dip a pancake into the water and leave for a few seconds, remove and drain on kitchen paper. Lay flat and place a little of each ingredient on the pancake. Fold the sides over to enclose the filling, and roll forward to make a cylinder. Arrange four spring rolls per serving on a plate and decorate with sprigs of coriander and mint and four curls of lettuce. Serve with the dipping sauce.

Wild Rice Salad with Mushroom Vinaigrette, Caramelized Onion, Tomatoes and Feta Cheese

Serves 2

Preparation: 15 minutes.
Cooking: 40 minutes, plus optional 30 minutes cooling

100g wild rice
350ml cold water
1 tsp salt
1 Spanish onion
2 tbsp olive oil
1 tbsp brown sugar
1 tbsp red wine vinegar
100g mushrooms
1 plump garlic clove

1 tbsp chopped flat-leaf
  parsley
juice of half a large lemon
10 baby plum or cherry
  tomatoes
2 tbsp chopped mint
100g feta cheese
salt and freshly milled black
  pepper

People often call wild rice the caviare of grains, and it's certainly as black and glossy as the finest beluga. Like caviare, its quality varies, but in this case the best grain is the longest.

Actually, wild rice isn't rice at all: it's the seed of a water grass that grows wild around the lakes and rivers of North America. For hundreds of years it was the staple diet of Sioux Indians and other native tribes. They called it manoomin and gathered it by hand, but today wild rice is cultivated on a huge scale, particularly in California and Minnesota.

For best results this long, needle-like grain needs slow cooking. It always seems disappointing that its shape and colour are changed in the process – it splits and puffs and quadruples in volume – but the good thing is that, unlike with regular rice, it's impossible to end up with claggy stodge. Be warned, though: while it's cooking it smells as if you have a stew of old socks and mouldy grass on the go.

Because wild rice is pricey, and because it's so distinctive looking, it's often used as a 'garnish' rather than as a key ingredient. I prefer to eat it less often and get the full benefit of its almost smoky flavour.

1. Wash the rice and place in a saucepan with the water and salt. Bring to the boil, lower the temperature, cover the pan and cook at a simmer until all the water is absorbed and the rice has burst and swelled. This will take 30–40 minutes.

2. Peel, halve and finely slice the onion. Place a medium saucepan over a high flame, add ½ tablespoon of olive oil and stir in the onions. Stir-fry, maintaining a fierce heat, for 6–7 minutes until the onions wilt and edges brown. Sprinkle over the sugar and stir-fry, lowering the heat slightly, until the sugar dissolves. Add the vinegar and leave to stew for 30 minutes until pleasantly soft and gooey.

3. Finely slice the mushrooms. Peel the garlic and finely chop. Heat ½ tablespoon of olive oil in a frying pan and cook the mushrooms with the garlic and parsley, tossing them around until the mushrooms are tender and brown – this takes a couple of minutes.

4. Pour the lemon juice into a salad bowl, season with salt and pepper then whisk in the remaining 1 tablespoon of olive oil. Add the mushrooms, the wild rice and fork through the onions. If you have time, leave the salad to macerate and cool for 30 minutes before adding the tomatoes (halved), the mint and feta cut into small chunks.

Comfort Suppers

Monday is comfort-grub day in the *Standard*. Most of the dishes, such as onion macaroni cheese with roast tomatoes, and bangers and mash with onion gravy, are old friends. Others, such as leeks mornay with prosciutto and a sort of soufflé with taleggio and mash, and smoked salmon with potato and dill, are new takes on continental favourites. The common denominator here is that the food is soothing and delicious, creamy and luscious, without being too rich or packed with protein. This is family food to eat on your lap, food for comfort.

A Sort of Soufflé with Taleggio and Mash

Serves 2–3   *Preparation: 15 minutes. Cooking: 30 minutes*

1 large shallot
1 garlic clove
50g butter
600g (approx.) cold leftover
   mashed potato
2 eggs

250g block taleggio cheese
freshly grated nutmeg
2 tbsp freshly grated
   Parmesan
salt and freshly milled black
   pepper

The universal leftover must be mashed potato, and there are times when I think it would make an excellent subject for a little book; in fact I'd love to write one. This is a great supper dish and it can be adapted to whatever quantity of mash you've got; you could make it in individual portions or in an earthenware gratin dish, as I did, to feed as many as your dish allows.

All you do is soften a diced shallot and a clove of garlic in butter for a couple of minutes and fold it into the mashed potato along with one or more beaten eggs and a generous seasoning of salt, black pepper and nutmeg. If you bother to separate the eggs and fold the whisked egg whites into the mash after the yolk is incorporated, the mixture will be lighter and even more bouffant – but I didn't bother.

Next, I diced a block of taleggio cheese – its tough skin removed – and mixed it with the potato. This is then piled into a well-buttered gratin dish, forked up decoratively, and generously dusted with grated Parmesan and dotted with butter.

It's baked in a hot oven for about 25 minutes until splendidly puffed and the edges, and most of the top, are gorgeously crusted and golden brown. When you spoon a portion on to your plate, the inside is laced with molten cheese and it looks and smells extremely appetizing – which it is! This soufflé is good enough to eat on its own, or with a salad made with floppy lettuce, but it is possibly best with a poached egg or two so that the soft yolk can mingle with the mash.

Other perfect additions, alone or with the egg, are roast tomatoes (halved, smeared with oil, seasoned and cooked at the same time in the bottom of the oven), and a few boiled leeks, split and dressed with vinaigrette. Come to think of it, with or without the cheese, this would go well with just about anything. Hot or cold.

1. Pre-heat the oven to 400F/200C/gas mark 6.

2. Peel and finely dice the shallot and garlic. Use a knob of the butter from the given amount, melt it in a frying pan over a medium-low flame and gently cook the shallot, tossing it about for 3–4 minutes until softened but not coloured. Tip on to a plate to cool.

3. Put the mash into a large mixing bowl (if you're making mash for this, let it cool first). Whisk the eggs and pour on to the potato. Season generously with salt, pepper and nutmeg and mix thoroughly with a fork to begin with, then a spoon. Now mix in the cooled shallot and garlic.

4. Remove the skin of the taleggio and cut it into chunks (it's best straight from the fridge or it's too soft and unmanageable) and mix the cheese evenly into the mash.

5. Use half the remaining butter to grease generously an earthenware dish (mine was 25½cm in diameter and 5cm deep) and spoon in the mash. Smooth over the top and fork up to make plenty of edges. Sprinkle over the Parmesan and dot with the remaining butter. Bake for 25 minutes or until crusted and golden. Eat.

Bangers and Mash with Onion Gravy

Serves 4   *Preparation: 25 minutes. Cooking: 45 minutes*

4 medium onions
small knob of butter
very scant tbsp cooking oil
1 tbsp flour
half a glass of red wine if
   available
300ml meat stock
1 tsp tomato purée
1 tsp English mustard
dash of Worcester sauce

900g floury potatoes such as
   King Edward
75g butter
approx. 150ml hot milk
salt, freshly milled black
   pepper and nutmeg
1 tbsp cooking oil
12 top-grade (minimum 80
   per cent meat) sausages

Succulent, plump, meaty sausages cooked until they're brown and crusty. Who can resist them sizzling in the frying pan?

There are hundreds of varieties of sausage. Antony and Araminta Hippersley-Coxe list more than 500 in their exhaustive Book Of Sausages (Victor Gollancz). And Martin Heap sells thirty-five flavours at Simply Sausages (93 Berwick Street, W1: tel 0171 287 3482). His are as close as you'll get to home-made sausages, made with high-quality natural ingredients and no additives.

Martin specializes in British regionals like my favourites Kentish Hop (pork, hops and real ale) and Scrumpy (pork with apple and rough cider). But the star of his gourmet list – guinea fowl and foie gras, if you please – really isn't a big fat porky. He also offers vegetarian selections, some of which are gluten-free.

Meat sausages, including Sainsbury's rather good Mulligatawny sausages (80 per cent pork with fresh ginger, green chillies and garlic), go well with buttery, well-whipped mashed potato and lashings of highly seasoned, thick, dark brown gravy.

So here's my version of these two much-abused national favourites. It's worth pointing out that good-quality bangers don't have to be pricked.

1. Peel, halve and finely slice the onions. Heat the butter and oil to sizzling in a saucepan and stir in the onions. Let them brown in patches. This will take about 10 minutes. Then turn down the heat. Season, cover the pan and cook for 30 minutes. Remove the lid, turn up the heat and evaporate any juices. Sift the flour into the onions, stir thoroughly and beat in the wine, if using, and stock with a wooden spoon. Establish a simmer, stir in the tomato purée, mustard and Worcester sauce, and cook for a couple more minutes.

2. Peel the potatoes and cut them into even-sized chunks. Put the potatoes in cold water and bring them to the boil. Add salt and simmer until tender, about 20 minutes. Drain and mash the potatoes to get rid of all lumps. It's worth buying a mouli légumes to do this. Adjust the seasoning, pour in 100ml of hot milk and the butter and, using a wooden spoon, beat the potatoes for as long as your arm can stand. Rest and do it again. Adjust the consistency by adding more milk. Dust with nutmeg.

3. While the potatoes are cooking, heat 1 tablespoon of oil in a large frying pan and start cooking the sausages over a moderate flame. This will take about 12–15 minutes, and the sausages are ready when plump, firm and nicely crusty and brown. Serve the sausages with the onion gravy and a big scoop of mashed potato.

Lamb Kidney Lash-Up

Serves 1   *Preparation: 10 minutes. Cooking: 15 minutes*

1 scant tbsp oil or butter
2 small red onions
1 garlic clove
1 large or two normal-
    sized very fresh lamb's
    kidneys
1 medium courgette
1 tsp Dijon mustard

glass of red or white wine or
    2 tbsp red wine vinegar
    diluted with water
generous squirt tomato
    ketchup
1 tbsp finely chopped parsley
salt and freshly milled black
    pepper

It's not very often that scanning the butcher's window reveals a forgotten ingredient that looks so good you have to buy it. That was the case for me recently, while I waited in line hoping for inspiration. All the usual stuff was there, you know the sort of thing: the ever-expanding choice of minced meat, the many cuts of chicken – supreme, legs, thighs and, at my butcher, fresh chicken livers – the dainty lamb chops, the lamb for stewing and roasting, the dark-red venison and huge slabs of beef (still his speciality) waiting to be cut into steaks. Then, of course, there are the sausages. These are his other speciality and lately he's added ostrich, which lines up with venison, lamb and mint, wild boar, Cumberland and Toulouse, and countless other ways with pork.

It's absolutely ages since I've bought any kidneys and I can't remember when I last positively noticed them on the butcher's slab. Recently, soon after the shop had opened for business, I was tempted by the most perfect-looking lamb's kidneys. I usually buy them in their suet jackets but these sat plump and glossy, and quite irresistible. I bought two and cooked them separately in the following way; one for my teenage son who thinks he hates all 'slimy' meat, and one for me.

1. Peel and halve the onions. Slice them through root and shoot. Peel the garlic and finely chop. Trim the courgette and cut into ½cm diagonal slices. Slice the kidney in ½cm-thick pennies, cutting round the white 'core'.

2. Use a wok or thin frying pan to heat the oil or butter and cook the onions, stir-frying over a medium heat until wilted. This takes about 5 minutes. Add the garlic and cored and sliced kidney, tossing around until all the pieces of meat change colour. Add the courgette slices, toss around a bit more, then add the wine. Let it sizzle up and reduce a little then stir in the mustard and ketchup. Cook on, seasoning generously with salt and pepper, letting the sauce thicken and reduce slightly, until the kidneys are cooked but still bouncy to the touch and the courgettes are al dente. This takes a matter of minutes.

Pile over a mound of cooked rice or next to some boiled potatoes, sprinkle with the parsley and serve with peas.

Cauliflower Cheese and Roast Tomatoes with Lamb Chops

Serves 4   *Preparation: 30 minutes. Cooking: 40 minutes*

3 small onions
500ml milk
1 bay leaf
6 black peppercorns
40g butter
1 heaped tbsp flour
200g mature Cheddar
1 large cauliflower

3 tbsp home-made
    breadcrumbs
8 lamb cutlets
4 large plum or marmande
    tomatoes
1 tbsp cooking oil
salt and freshly milled black
    pepper

A few years ago, when Delia Smith's *Complete Illustrated Cookery Course* was published, I was granted an interview with her. We talked and talked, touching on her waitressing job at Le Chef which got her going on her phenomenal career, her favourite restaurants, and about her postbag, which, in those pre-lemongrass and cranberry days, was confined to tips on making gravy, cooking rice, getting meringues to rise, and pastry making.

At the end, I asked her for an easy supper idea. This is it: lamb chops ('crispy and the meat brown') laid over chopped onion with mint sauce in the summer and redcurrant jelly in the winter.

Any vegetables would go well with this but I decided on cauliflower cheese and roast tomatoes, both of which can be cooked in the oven at the same time as the chops.

This way of cooking the chops means they won't be pink; if that's the way you like them, then it would be better to cook them quickly over a fierce heat in a frying pan so the skin and fat get a chance to crisp while the meat inside stays rosy.

1. Peel and slice one of the onions. Place in a saucepan with the milk, peppercorns, bay leaf and a pinch of salt. Bring slowly to the boil, simmer very gently for 5 minutes, turn off the heat and cover the pan.

2. Pre-heat the oven to 400F/200C/gas mark 6. Put a large pan of water on to boil. Use a little of the butter to smear a dish for the cauliflower.

3. Trim away the huge leafy stalk of the cauliflower and cut out a triangular core. Cut the cauliflower into even-sized florets.

4. When the pan of water is boiling, add 1 teaspoon of salt and fling in the cauliflower. Bring back to the boil, cover the pan and cook for 4 minutes. Drain immediately, saving most of the cauliflower water.

5. Melt the butter in the cauliflower pan, stir in the flour and strain over the milk and 4 tablespoons of cauliflower water, using a wire whisk to get rid of lumps as it comes to the boil. Simmer very gently for a few minutes then stir in most of the cheese. Turn off the heat and mix in the cauliflower before tipping everything into the prepared dish. Even the surface and sprinkle over the breadcrumbs and reserved cheese.

6. Chop the remaining two onions, spread out in an oven dish and cover with the cutlets. Season with salt and pepper.

7. Halve the tomatoes, lay out in an oven dish, smear with oil and season. Place the cutlets and cauliflower on the top shelf of the oven, the tomatoes below. Turn the cutlets after 15 minutes, changing everything around if you think the cauliflower is browning too quickly.

8 Serve the cutlets with the mushy onions and juices. I must admit that I like mint sauce *and* redcurrant jelly.

Eggs Benedict

Serves 2   *Preparation: 10 minutes. Cooking: 15 minutes*

4 rashers rindless streaky
   bacon
2 English muffins
4 large very fresh free-range
   eggs
splash of vinegar

For the hollandaise sauce:
2 large very fresh free-range
   egg yolks
175g unsalted butter
juice of half a lemon
salt and freshly milled black
   pepper
½ tbsp finely chopped parsley

Eggs Benedict is the quintessential brunch dish and not something for calorie counters or cholesterol watchers to consider too often.

It's a wonderfully over-the-top combination of toasted muffin topped with either ham or bacon (I prefer the textural contrast and more assertive flavour of bacon) and soft poached eggs. Its crowning glory is hollandaise sauce, which is made with more butter than seems decent and yet more eggs.

Once upon a time, before the egg crisis and our obsession with low-fat food, hollandaise was everyone's favourite sauce, particularly when someone else made it.

It shares, along with soufflés, pâté, rice and gravy, an unfair reputation for being impossible to get right. I'm not going to claim that my recipe is foolproof, but I learned this method from a chef friend many years ago and it hasn't let me down – yet. Only the freshest and best eggs you can find will do for eggs Benedict.

The only thing to serve with eggs Benedict is a Bloody Mary. I like mine highly spiced with Tabasco and Worcester sauce, with a generous seasoning of celery salt, lemon juice and black pepper. It must be served very cold with plenty of ice. The traditional garnish is celery.

1. Grill the bacon until evenly crisp on both sides and drain on kitchen paper. Keep warm in a low oven. Split the muffins ready for toasting (either in the toaster, or leave the grill lit from cooking the bacon).

2. Half-fill a medium-sized saucepan with water, add the vinegar and put on to boil. Half-fill a second small pan with water and establish a very gentle simmer.

3. Now begin the hollandaise. Place the slab of butter in a small pan over a medium flame and melt completely. Remove from the heat and leave to settle for about 30 seconds before skimming away the white scum that will form on the surface.

Meanwhile whisk the egg yolks with ½ tablespoon of water in a bowl until it thickens and froths, then place the bowl over the pan of barely simmering water and keep whisking continuously as it quickly thickens. Remove from the heat and pour on the butter in a thin stream, whisking constantly as you pour until it resembles mayonnaise. Finally, whisk in the lemon juice and season with salt.

4. Crack an egg into a cup and slip it into the simmering vinegared water, adding the other three eggs in the same way. Cook at a gentle roll for 2–2½ minutes until evenly coagulated. Remove each egg with a slotted spoon and drain on kitchen paper.

5. Toast the muffins. Put two muffin halves on each plate, cut the bacon slices in half and arrange on top. Carefully lay the eggs on top. Spoon over the hollandaise, season with black pepper and sprinkle with parsley. Eat at once.

Jansson's Temptation

Serves 6   *Preparation: 20 minutes. Cooking: 60 minutes*

3 very large onions

2 × 50g cans of anchovies in
    oil or 115g can of Swedish
    anchovies

900g potatoes (waxy variety
    are best but any will do)

300ml double cream (or half
    double and half single
    cream)

freshly milled black pepper

3 tbsp home-made
    breadcrumbs

4 tbsp butter

Jansson's Temptation is a speciality, and has been for twenty years, of Anna Hegarty's delightfully idiosyncratic Swedish restaurant, Anna's Place, in Mildmay Park, N1, and this was where I first fell in love with it.

This Swedish dish is made with my two favourite ingredients, potatoes and onions. Grated potatoes and finely sliced onions, interspersed with a lattice of anchovy, are layered in a buttered casserole dish, covered with cream and baked until the vegetables are tender and the anchovy has dispersed its salty seasoning. I always make this dish with anchovies canned in olive oil, but to be authentic it should be made with Swedish anchovies which have a softer, mellower flavour and are preserved in water, vinegar, sugar and herbs. They can be bought from the Swedish Deli (369 King Street, W6, 0181 563 9211) and a 115g tin is just the right quantity for Jansson's Temptation. If you'd like to try the dish before you have a go at making it, this café/deli will sell you a takeaway portion.

This is an excellent recipe to know about because, provided you can lay your hands on some cream, it can be conjured up easily, leaving you free to do something else. Beer, incidentally, perhaps with a glass of cold schnapps as a chaser, is the perfect accompaniment to this moreish and satisfying dish.

1. Pre-heat the oven to 425F/220C/gas mark 7.

2. Peel, halve and slice the onions very, very thinly: this is important. Drain the anchovies and split lengthways – if using Swedish anchovies, retain the juice to add to the cream.

3. Use half the butter to butter liberally a large gratin dish or deep casserole.

4. Peel the potatoes and grate them (they are not rinsed; the starch adds texture and holds the dish together), working quickly because they will discolour. Depending on the dish you are using, make one or two layers beginning with potato, followed by a lattice of anchovy, onions and potatoes. Season each layer lightly with black pepper. When you've finished, press the mixture down firmly and smooth the surface.

5. Heat the cream, adding the liquid from the can if using Swedish anchovies, and when it has reached boiling point pour over the dish: the potatoes should be glimpsed, not smothered.

6. Season again with black pepper, sprinkle over the breadcrumbs, dot with the remaining butter and bake for 30 minutes. Lower the heat to 400F/200C/gas mark 6 and cook for another 30 minutes. Serve with a green salad. Leftovers are good cold and are excellent for a packed lunch or autumn picnic.

Kedgeree

Serves 4   *Preparation: 15 minutes. Cooking: 30 minutes*

1 large onion
knob of butter
½ tsp ground turmeric
450g basmati rice
450g smoked haddock
300ml milk
4 black peppercorns
1 bay leaf

25g butter
1 tsp curry powder
1 scant level tbsp flour
75ml cream
juice of half a lemon
3 hard-boiled eggs, peeled
2 tbsp finely chopped flat-leaf
    parsley

Kedgeree started out as a highly spiced lentil and rice dish called khichri. When the British arrived in India we adopted khichri as a breakfast dish and set about adapting it to our tastes. According to David Burton in *The Raj at Table* (Faber & Faber), we replaced the dal with flaked fresh fish, 'dropped the spices, added hard-boiled egg, anglicized the name, and kedgeree was born'.

Sadly, kedgeree has fallen out of favour as a breakfast dish but is finding its way on to fashionable menus for lunch and dinner. Whatever time of day, at its best, when the rice is tender, moist and creamy, the seasoning subtle yet haunting and smoked haddock is the chosen fish, this is perfect comfort food.

The association with smoked haddock is not, as I'd thought, strictly traditional and came later, by fluke. Apparently it happened in the 18th century, when the arrival of the dish in Britain coincided with a new communications network – particularly a coach connection with Findon, home of today's Finnan haddock.

Usually kedgeree is made by cooking rice which has been fried with onion and coloured and flavoured with turmeric and curry powder. The rice is then mixed with poached and flaked smoked haddock and decorated with boiled egg and chopped parsley. When I made it this way the result was pleasant, but dry, despite the cream and butter I'd added for moistness. Apologies, then, to the purists: to get the full comfort factor I've reverted to my somewhat unorthodox version of kedgeree.

1. Peel and finely chop the onion. Rinse the rice until the water runs clean. Heat the knob of butter in a large saucepan and fry the onion for a few minutes until lightly golden. Stir in the turmeric and then the rice, cooking until the rice is lightly glazed.

Pour on 900ml water, bring to the boil, turn down to establish a gentle simmer, cover the pan and leave for at least 15 minutes until the rice is tender and the water absorbed.

2. Meanwhile, cut the haddock into manageable pieces which will fit snugly in a pan, add the bay leaf and peppercorns and pour over the milk. Simmer for 10 minutes. Strain the milk into a jug and when the fish is cool enough to handle lift the flesh off the skin and flake in big chunks into a bowl.

3. Melt the 25g butter in a small pan, stir in the curry powder and cook for a couple of minutes before adding the flour. Strain over the poaching milk, stirring constantly to avoid lumps (a globe whisk is useful) and simmer very gently for about 10 minutes. Add the cream and bring back to simmer.

Stir in the lemon juice. Turn off the heat and add the fish, stirring gently so as not to break up the pieces. Gently fold the sauce into the rice and transfer the kedgeree to a warm shallow serving dish.

Sprinkle over the parsley and decorate with slices of boiled egg.

Hachis Parmentier

Serves 4   *Preparation: 20 minutes. Cooking: 55 minutes*

1 tbsp cooking oil
25g butter
8 rashers streaky bacon
2 medium onions
1 celery stick
2 plump garlic cloves
1 bay leaf
1 tbsp fresh thyme leaves
4 tbsp chopped flat-leaf
    parsley
500g minced lamb
50g fine white breadcrumbs
    soaked in 4 tbsp milk
2 tbsp tomato purée

salt and freshly milled black
    pepper

For the mash:
1kg floury potatoes
150ml–300ml hot milk
40g butter
generous pinch freshly grated
    nutmeg

To finish:
50g grated Gruyère
50g fine white breadcrumbs
40g butter

It's extraordinary that so many people think shepherd's pie should be made with minced beef. It seems obvious, when you think about it, that as shepherds herd sheep, their pies would be made with lamb; and tracing the dish back, as many food writers have done, I found the original recipes were a way of 'using up' left-over cooked mutton.

There isn't the same confusion with the French version of the dish because traditionally, and indisputably, it is made with the chopped remains of the pot-au-feu. And that means beef. The Parmentier part of the title comes from Antoine-Auguste Parmentier, the fellow who introduced the potato to France in the 18th century and whose name is connected with all manner of potato dishes.

And unlike our shepherd's and cottage pies, which almost always have only a potato topping, the French edition has a layer of potato underneath as well, and the top is given a crusty gratin finish with a layer of breadcrumbs and cheese.

This recipe is something of a mongrel, if that's a word you can use to describe a dish: my Hachis Parmentier is made with fresh minced lamb instead of beef but seasoned *à la française* with garlic, plenty of fresh thyme and flat-leafed parsley and onions.

1. Dice the bacon. Peel and finely chop the onion. Trim, finely chop and wash the celery. Peel and dice the garlic. Melt half the butter and oil in a large frying pan or heavy-based casserole and fry the bacon until crisp. Add the onion, garlic, celery, thyme, bay leaf and half the parsley to the pan. Season with a little salt and pepper and cook over a low heat until the vegetables are tender. Transfer to a plate.

2. Add the remaining butter and oil to the pan and stir in the meat. Cook briskly, stirring until it changes colour, then return the vegetables with the tomato purée, breadcrumbs and milk. Leave to cook very gently for 15 minutes and stir in the remaining parsley.

3. Meanwhile, peel the potatoes, cut into similar-sized chunks and cook until tender. Drain and mash with the butter then beat in enough milk to make a fluffy but firm mash. Season with nutmeg and spoon one-third of the mash into a buttered shallow oven-proof dish. Cover with the meat and top with the remaining mash, spreading it evenly with a fork. Sprinkle over the cheese and breadcrumbs and dot with any remaining butter. Cook in a hot oven (350F/180C/gas mark 4) for 30 minutes. Serve with a garlicky green salad, French bread and le ketchup.

Leeks Mornay with Prosciutto

Serves 4   *Preparation: 40 minutes. Cooking: 20 minutes*

6 medium leeks (approx. 1kg)
1 bay leaf
4 black peppercorns
generous pinch of salt
500ml milk
12 slices prosciutto or 24 slices
   thin ham

40g butter
3 tbsp flour
100g good-quality Cheddar
   cheese
nutmeg
small knob of butter
2 tbsp Parmesan cheese

The secret of perfectly cooked leeks, a chef once told me, is to drop them into plenty of vigorously boiling salted water and cook them until just tender to the point of a knife. That way, in theory, the leeks don't get water-logged and their delicate flavour and colour won't be lost to the cooking pot. Another solution is to cook them in a steamer.

Steaming is perfect for this recipe because, once cooked, the leeks are cut into big chunks, bundled up in a slice of ham and baked under a thick, cheesy blanket. It's a refinement of a dish that I've been cooking for years and have eaten at countless bistros in France.

Usually, whole leeks, or chicory, are wrapped in ham or bacon, then covered with a béchamel sauce and browned in the top of the oven. Too often this superior comfort food is ruined by watery, overcooked, slimy leeks which leech into their sauce. It's also always struck me that there's never enough ham, and, anyway, however sharp the knife, the leeks are difficult to cut into manageable mouthfuls.

In this version everything is put to rights: the leeks are tender but still firm, you can't run out of ham and the cheese sauce is thick, creamy and richly flavoured. It goes particularly well with mashed potatoes and sprouts or finely shredded and briefly boiled Savoy cabbage.

1. Trim away the roots and the tough, dark-green ends of the leeks. If necessary to fit your steamer or saucepan, cut the leeks in half. Rinse and leave them to soak in cold water.

2. Bring the steamer or a large saucepan of water to the boil, add salt, and cook the leeks for 8–12 minutes. Test with the point of a knife; they should feel firm but not crunchy. Remove from the steamer. If cooking in water, drain them, green-end down.

3. Place the bay leaf, peppercorns, salt and milk in a pan and bring the milk to the boil. Simmer gently for 5 minutes, then cover the pan and turn off the heat.

4. Use the small knob of butter to grease a shallow ceramic gratin-type dish.

5. Cut each leek into four pieces approximately 3½cm in size. If using prosciutto, cut the slices in half. Wrap each piece of leek in a piece of ham and pack them in a single layer in the dish.

6. Grate the Cheddar.

7. Melt the butter and stir in the flour to make a stiff roux. Pour the milk through a sieve into the roux. As you pour, beat continuously with a whisk or wooden spoon to get rid of any lumps. Simmer gently for 8 minutes, then stir in the cheese, and cook until it's melted. Pour the sauce over the leeks. Season with grated nutmeg, then sprinkle with the Parmesan.

8. Cook in a pre-heated oven (350F/180C/gas mark 4) for 20 minutes until the top is crusty and bubbling around the edges.

Middle Eastern Shepherd's Pie

Serves 4   *Preparation: 30 minutes. Cooking: 55 minutes*

750g potatoes
2 tbsp cooking oil
2 tbsp pine kernels
3 medium onions
3 garlic cloves
pinch saffron stamens
    dissolved in 1 tbsp boiling
    water
1 tsp ground cinnamon
750g minced lamb
juice of half a lemon

approx. 225g canned
    chickpeas, rinsed
300ml chicken stock
half a bay leaf
2 tbsp chopped parsley
2 tbsp mint
125g feta cheese
1–2 tbsp olive oil
salt and freshly milled black
    pepper

Not an April Fool but a variation on a dish that's one of many on hold at the moment for most people.

I've always made shepherd's pie with minced beef, which of course is really cottage pie. I don't have a standard recipe; it's more a question of adding anything I think will help add interest to what can be a tasteless, dull dish. A generous slug of red wine and a long, slow simmer before assembling the dish always seem to help.

As I set out to make a lamb shepherd's pie I found myself reaching for the flavourings and ingredients I often team with minced lamb. Out came the pine kernels, a lemon, garlic, mint and flat-leaf parsley, more onions than usual and extra garlic. Saffron was next and then came cinnamon. Quite why I'm not sure, but minced lamb doesn't seem to go as far as minced beef. Half a can of chickpeas seemed an appropriate ingredient to lend bulk as well as interest.

Instead of the usual mashed potatoes I covered the pie with big chunks of pre-boiled potatoes and dribbled them with olive oil. Reinventing favourite dishes is a dodgy business: the whole point about them is that they are reassuringly familiar. This pie provides the all-important comfort-food factor with just enough spin on it to excite the jaded palate.

1. Peel the potatoes, rinse and cut into even-sized chunks. Cook in salted water until tender; allow 15–20 minutes. Drain.

2. Heat a splash of cooking oil in a frying pan and stir-fry the pine kernels until golden. Drain on absorbent paper.

3. Peel, halve and slice the onions. Peel and slice the garlic in thin rounds.

4. Heat the rest of the cooking oil in a casserole dish, add the onions and garlic and cook over a medium heat for 10 minutes, stirring a couple of times. Sprinkle on the saffron, cinnamon, half the mint, half the parsley and bay leaf. Mix in the minced lamb. Cook, stirring a couple of times, until the meat is evenly browned. Squeeze over the lemon juice, add the chickpeas and stock and boil hard for 10–15 minutes or until almost all the liquid has been concentrated and absorbed.

5. Stir in the feta and then the pine kernels and reserved herbs. Taste and adjust the seasoning with salt and pepper and possibly more lemon juice.

6. Pour into a suitable ovenproof dish. Top with the drained potato chunks. Dribble with the olive oil.

7. Cook in a hot oven (400F/200C/gas mark 6) for 20 minutes until the potato edges are nicely crusted.

Onion Macaroni Cheese with Roast Tomatoes

Serves 4   *Preparation: 35 minutes. Cooking: 15 minutes*

4 tomatoes

pinch of sugar

1 tsp olive oil

350g large macaroni

1 Spanish onion

3 medium leeks

large knob of butter

For the cheese sauce:

25g butter

1 heaped tbsp flour

425ml milk

150ml double cream

1 heaped tsp English mustard

1 bay leaf

100g mature Cheddar

packet of chives (at least
    4 tbsp)

4 tbsp freshly grated
    Parmesan

salt and freshly milled black
    pepper

Easy, quick and familiar, but a little bit different. Perfect Monday night food.

This macaroni cheese isn't made with the usual tiny macaroni: instead I've used a big chunky version found at my local Cypriot grocery, the ever resourceful Adamous of Chiswick High Road.

Any fat tubular lengths of pasta will do, or you could use large shells or circular noodles. The cheese sauce is perked up with masses of chives and English mustard, then mixed with buttery strands of soft onion and just-tender chunks of leek.

When everything is cooked and mixed together it's eaten as it is, risotto-style, dusted with freshly grated Parmesan cheese and a sharply dressed tomato salad on the side.

However, it's more Monday nightish poured into a shallow

baking dish, topped with grated Parmesan and popped into a hot oven until the top turns brown and crusty.

Cook the tomato halves separately while the oven heats up for the macaroni, and then finish them off while it's cooking.

1. Turn the oven on to 400F/200C/gas mark 6. Slice the tomatoes in half across their circumference. Rub top and bottom with olive oil and place, cut side up, on a baking tray. Season with salt, pepper and sugar. Place near the top of the oven.

2. Cook the pasta according to packet instructions, probably 15 minutes in boiling water, and drain.

3. Peel and slice the onion. Melt the knob of butter in a spacious pan and cook the onion over a gentle heat for 6 minutes.

4. Trim the leeks and slice the white and pale-green parts into 2½cm-thick chunks. Rinse under cold running water. Add the leeks to the onion, give everything a good stir, cover the pan and cook for a further 6 minutes.

5. Make the sauce by melting the butter then stirring in the flour to make a thick paste. Mix in the mustard, add the bay leaf, a pinch of salt and freshly milled pepper. Use a wooden spoon to incorporate the milk and cream, stirring briskly as it comes up to the boil to get rid of any lumps. Simmer gently for 6 minutes.

6. Grate the Cheddar and stir into the sauce. Add the chives.

7. Mix the pasta, onion mixture and sauce together and pour into a shallow baking dish. Scatter over the Parmesan.

8. Move the tomatoes to a low shelf and replace with the macaroni. Cook for 15 minutes until the top is golden and crusty in places.

Serve straight from the oven, giving each serving two tomato halves.

The Perfect Chip Butty

Serves 1   *Preparation: 15 minutes. Cooking: 20 minutes*

clean groundnut oil for
   deep-frying
2 large floury potatoes such as
   King Edward
2 × 15cm lengths of authentic
   baguette

salt-free French butter
dollop Hellman's mayonnaise
sea salt flakes (not crystals)
   and freshly milled black
   pepper
½ lemon

Chip butties have been a bit non-U for years, so it's a relief to see one on the menu of the Anglesea Arms in Wingate Road, W6. Dan Evans's choice of bread is what can only be described as controversial. The classic chip butty is made with doorsteps, hewn from a bog-standard white loaf. Personally I like this contrast of flabby cold bread against hot, crisp chips, yet there are times when all I crave is a chip butty made with Sunblest or some other processed bread: you just can't beat the way the bread goes almost slimy and melts against the chips. But have you ever tried a chip butty made with really good butter spread on thick slices of exceedingly fresh wholemeal?

The sort of bread you use is a matter of taste, and so too is the seasoning. Salt is essential and, for my money, so too is black pepper. Sometimes I douse the butty with vinegar – and it's got to be malt – or take a tip from Belgium, and add mayonnaise. And what about tomato ketchup? Should it go inside the butty (with vinegar?) or be kept separate?

These important points fade into (almost) insignificance when compared with the quality of the chip. To get what I think is vital for all the right textures, I favour the British chunky-cut. And I don't like a hint of grease on those crisp edges that cover fluffy floury insides, but I do want the chips hot from the pan. Herewith, then, after much experimentation, is my recipe for perfect chips and my current favourite way of making a chip butty.

1. Half-fill a suitable pan or electric deep-fat fryer with oil and gently heat to 300F/150C/gas mark 2.
2. Slit the baguette lengthways on one side, butter generously and smear one side with mayo.
3. Meanwhile peel the potatoes and cut lengthways to your preferred thickness. Place in a colander and wash under cold running water to get rid of starch. Drain and wrap in a tea towel to dry. The chips are going to be cooked twice. The first stage, at a lower temperature, cooks but doesn't colour the potato. The chips can be kept in this state for several hours, overnight if necessary. The finishing off is done at a higher temperature and gives the chips their colour and crisps them up. For both stages it's important not to crowd the pan.
4. Fry the chips for 6–7 minutes until tender but uncoloured. Lift out the basket and allow to drain; if you're doing this in batches, transfer to a plate and cook the rest of the chips. To finish them off, increase the temperature to 350F/180C and continue cooking for between 45 seconds and 3 minutes. It might be wise to experiment with one chip because potatoes cook up differently at different times of the year. If the chips refuse to crisp, remove the basket from the oil, raise the temperature again and cook for a third time. Drain on absorbent kitchen paper, sprinkle with salt and season with black pepper.
5. Load the chips into the bread. Squeeze over a little lemon juice and eat, dipping stray chips into tomato ketchup.

Smoked Salmon with Potato and Dill

Serves 6   *Preparation: 35 minutes. Cooking: 30 minutes*

1.2kg medium potatoes
150g spring onions
40g butter
165g smoked salmon
bunch fresh dill

4 large eggs
350ml milk
salt and freshly milled black
    pepper

There are times when you are not quite sure how many people you will be feeding and it's uncertain when you're going to eat.

Ideally, should there be latecomers or if you have made too much, you want something that won't suffer from being eaten lukewarm or cold the next day.

When I was faced with a situation like this recently, the only fresh food I had was a few eggs, some milk and butter, some spring onions, some fresh parsley and dill, a lettuce and a little smoked salmon.

I didn't have the energy to make pastry – smoked-salmon-and-dill quiche would have been an excellent solution – but I wanted something a bit special which wouldn't require much effort.

My solution was inspired by a Swedish dish called Lax Pudding; a kind of layer bake (a loathsome but apt description) made with fresh dill-marinated salmon and potatoes.

Using what I had, I made layers of sliced boiled potatoes, smoked salmon, dill and spring onions, and covered the dish with the eggs and milk.

It's child's play to prepare: all you have to do is slice the potatoes and onions, whisk the egg into the milk and put everything into a buttered dish.

While it cooks, the egg and milk set into a custard and make a lovely gooey, eggy background to the salmon and potatoes. The softened onions taste sweet and slightly of peas and dill's overpowering flavour dulls to just the right level.

If necessary, this dish can be kept waiting for hours before it goes into the oven – in the fridge, covered with transparent film, the egg and milk poured on at the last minute.

A simple green salad made with a floppy lettuce is the perfect accompaniment.

1. Peel the potatoes, rinse and cook in a pan of salted boiling water until tender to the point of a knife. Strain and set aside to cool while you attend to everything else.

2. Trim the spring onions and finely slice the white and pale-green parts. Pull the dill fronds off their stalks and roughly chop – you need at least 2 tablespoons, preferably 3. Slice the smoked salmon into long 2½cm-wide strips.

3. Use about one-third of the butter to grease generously a shallow ceramic dish approx. 25 × 20cm.

4. When the potatoes have cooled slightly cut into ½cm-thick slices. Cover the base of the dish with one-third of the potato slices and season with salt and pepper.

Sprinkle over half the spring onions, lay half the smoked salmon slices over the top and strew half the dill over the salmon. Season with black pepper. Make a second layer as before, then top with the last of the potatoes.

5. Whisk the eggs into the milk and pour over the dish; it won't entirely cover it, leaving the potato topping to get nicely crusty. Dot with the remaining butter, season again and bake for 30 minutes in a hot oven (400F/200C/gas mark 6).

Soubise Herb Gratin

Serves 4　　　　　　　*Preparation: 25 minutes. Cooking: 55 minutes*

4 Spanish onions
75g butter
175g basmati rice
1 wine glass (approx. 150ml) of
　dry white wine
300ml hot water
half a bay leaf
6 tbsp freshly grated
　Parmesan cheese

6 tbsp crème fraîche or
　double cream
small bunch of flat-leaf
　parsley
6 sage leaves
2 slices of stale bread
salt and freshly milled black
　pepper

Soubise is a name synonymous with onions and goes back to the 18th century when the chef to the Prince of Soubise invented a delicately flavoured onion sauce. He boiled the onions in water first, then added them to a béchamel sauce finished with cream; wonderful with fish or poached lamb.

This recipe could be puréed and turned into that sauce – thin it with milk or cream and then pass it through a sieve – and is a thick and creamy dish of braised onions and rice.

My soubise can be eaten on its own and goes well with most other vegetables, particularly grilled tomatoes, and with sausages, bacon and chicken. It also makes an excellent gratin and is a comforting meat-free supper.

Don't rush the cooking of the onions; it's important to cook them slowly in plenty of butter until tender without browning. Also, use basmati rice which retains its bite and fluffs into separate grains.

All you need with this is a salad of mixed green leaves or a chicory salad with a mustardy vinaigrette.

1. Peel, halve and finely slice the onions.

2. Melt most of the butter in a spacious heavy-bottomed saucepan with a tight-fitting lid. Stir in the onions, cover, and cook over a low heat for about 30 minutes or until the onions are tender but not browned. Stir once or twice.

3. Meanwhile, finely chop the parsley and the sage leaves and set aside in separate piles.

4. When the onions are ready, add the rice and a generous seasoning of salt. Raise the heat slightly and stir for 3–4 minutes. Pour in the wine, let it bubble up and then add the hot water and bay leaf. Bring to the boil, establish a simmer, stir once, then cover the pan and cook for 15–20 minutes until the liquid has been absorbed and the rice is tender.

5. Stir in most of the parsley and half the sage. Stir in 4 tablespoons of the Parmesan and the crème fraîche or double cream and adjust the seasoning with salt and pepper.

6. Butter a shallow gratin dish and tip in the onion rice.

7. Trim away the crusts of the bread, blitz in the food processor to make breadcrumbs and mix with the remaining cheese and herbs. Sprinkle over the top, dot with the last of the butter and place under the grill until the top is crusty and slightly charred in places. If you're making this in advance, pop it into a hot oven (400F/200C/gas mark 6) for about 15 minutes.

Spag Bol Florentine

Serves 4–6   *Preparation: 15 minutes. Cooking: 60 minutes*

1 tbsp cooking oil

40g butter

4 rashers streaky bacon

1 medium onion

2 medium carrots

2 sticks celery

450g minced lamb

250ml passata (or can of
puréed and sieved
tomatoes)

salt

250ml dry red wine

tsp nutmeg

150ml milk

100g spinach

25g butter

450g spaghetti

squeeze of lemon juice

freshly milled black pepper

Ragu, which is the proper name for the meat sauce in this ubiquitous dish, is described differently in just about every recipe.

My version is yet another hybrid and, sacrilege probably, it is made with minced lamb rather than beef. One of the important points that most authentic recipes have in common is allowing the sauce to cook for far longer than would seem necessary.

Marcella Hazan, the godmother of Italian recipe writing, suggests 3½ hours (though 5 hours, she says, would be better).

These authentic recipes result in a thicker and intensely savoury sauce, when the vegetables entirely disappear and the meat and tomato merge into a dark reddish-brown lotion with no distinctive characteristics.

One good thing about making ragu with lamb is that you seem to end up with this desired texture, colour and rich flavour within about an hour of cooking.

I took several tips from Ms Hazan's recipe in *The Classic Italian*

Cookbook and followed her advice about order of adding and cooking (to the point of almost total evaporation), first the wine, then the milk and tomatoes.

I had the idea of adding spinach – that's the Florentine bit – when I happened to have some that needed finishing up, and it works really well.

1. Dice the bacon. Heat the oil and butter in a heavy-bottomed pan. Fry the bacon and remove when crisp.
2. Peel and dice the onion and carrot. Trim the celery and finely chop. Add the onion to the pan and fry for a couple of minutes before adding the carrot and celery.
3. Cook for 2 minutes and add the lamb. Season with a generous pinch of salt and cook until the meat changes colour. Add the wine. Turn up the heat to medium-high and cook, stirring occasionally, until all the wine has evaporated.
4. Add the milk and nutmeg. Repeat, stirring frequently, and when the milk has almost entirely disappeared (it takes about ten minutes) add the passata.
5. Return the bacon to the pan. Bring to the boil then turn down low and cook at a gentle simmer, uncovered, for 35 minutes.
6. Meanwhile, wash the spinach. Drain and stuff into a second pan. Cover and cook over a low–medium heat, turning to get the top layer cooked, until floppy.

Drain in a colander and roughly chop against the side. Add the butter to the cooking pan, stir in the spinach and let everything amalgamate.

Stir into the ragu for the last 5 minutes of cooking.
7. Cook the spaghetti according to packet instructions.
8. Taste the ragu, adjusting the seasoning with salt, pepper and a squeeze of lemon juice. Serve in a dollop over the spaghetti.

Two-Haddock Fish Pie
with Minted Peas

Serves 6   *Preparation: 60 minutes. Cooking: 20 minutes*

1.8kg floury potatoes
900ml milk
1 medium onion
1 bay leaf
4 black peppercorns
4 tbsp flour
700g thick haddock fillet
450g smoked haddock

4 eggs
175g butter
1 dsp anchovy essence
½ tsp salt
freshly milled black pepper
leaves from a large bunch
   flat-leaf parsley

Carefully made fish pie is one of the best possible supper dishes. It should never include bones, and I like it made with a good ratio of fish to other texturally different ingredients. It works well with most fish – the mackerel family and probably squid are the exceptions – and a mixture of fish works well. This is my standard recipe which I sometimes liven up with a handful of peeled prawns or with big chunks of peeled tomato stirred into the sauce.

The perfect accompaniment to fish pie is a bowl of peas with plenty of freshly chopped mint and a knob of butter.

1. Peel and chop the onion and place it with the bay leaf, peppercorns and a pinch of salt in a saucepan with 700ml of the milk. Bring to the boil, establish a simmer and cook for 10 minutes. Turn off the heat, cover and leave for 15 minutes. Strain the milk over the fish which you've laid out, skin side down, in a single layer in a shallow pan or dish. Add a knob of butter and simmer, turning the fish after 5 minutes, and cook on for a few more minutes until the fish is lightly but not completely cooked. Lift the fish on to a large plate and leave to cool.

2. Meanwhile, peel the potatoes and cut them into even-sized chunks. Place the rinsed potatoes in a saucepan with the 4 eggs. Cover with water and cook until the water boils. Add the salt and cook at a brisk simmer until the potatoes are tender. This will take about 20 minutes. Drain. Remove the eggs and immediately crack and then peel them under cold running water. Set the eggs aside.

3. Heat 150ml milk with 50g butter in the potato cooking pan. Return the drained potatoes and mash, adding more milk if necessary, to make a firm mash. Top with a small knob of butter and cover with a napkin.

4. Make a sauce for the fish by melting 50g butter in a small pan. Stir in the flour then pour the fishy milk into the roux. As you pour, beat continuously with a whisk or wooden spoon to get rid of any lumps. Simmer gently for a few minutes. Season with black pepper and anchovy essence.

5. Ease the fish off the skin in chunks, taking care to remove bones, and put it in a large bowl. Chop the egg and add it to the bowl. Pick the leaves from the parsley stalks and chop them finely – you should have at least 3 tablespoons – and add to the bowl. Pour over the sauce and carefully mix around. Smear a large shallow dish with butter (mine was 36 × 23cm) and tip in the fish mixture. Top with the potato, smoothing and scraping the top with the prongs of a fork. Dot with butter and cook for 20 minutes at 400F/200C/gas mark 6, or until the top is nicely crusty and golden.

Suppers Without Meat

When you look at fashionable menus now, pitted as they are with choice after choice for dishes without meat, or glance in the chill counter of any supermarket, it's a shock to remember that less than ten years ago vegetarians were regarded as second-class citizens. I know that my cooking has changed over recent years, prompted as much by food scares as the price of properly reared meat, towards vegetarianism. Without making a conscious effort, I eat meat- and fish-free meals at least twice a week, sometimes more often.

Spinach and ricotta Parmesan pie with red salad and black olives, parsley potato gnocchi with sage butter and Parmesan, is the sort of food I'm talking about, and baked ratatouille with soft poached eggs and potato pithivier. These dishes are delicious in their own right, and are satisfying enough, in terms of texture and colour as well as flavour, that no one notices the lack of meat.

Baked Ratatouille with Soft Poached Eggs

Serves 4 (with enough ratatouille for 8)   *Preparation: 20 minutes.*
Cooking: 1 hour

1 large onion (approx. 300g)

4 garlic cloves

1 large red pepper (approx. 200g)

1 medium aubergine (approx. 300g)

3 medium courgettes (approx. 100g each)

8 ripe medium tomatoes

6 tbsp olive oil

1 bay leaf

3 sprigs of fresh thyme

salt and freshly milled black pepper

4 eggs

1 tbsp vinegar

2 tbsp your best olive oil

1 tbsp snipped chives

When ratatouille is good – and the ripeness of the vegetables is crucial here – it's fabulous. But too often it's a disappointing watery slop. I have only really enjoyed my own ratatouille since I discovered Michel Guerard's oven method in his book *Cuisine Minceur* (published here in 1977). I also like his way of gentrifying the dish with thin rather than chunky-chopped vegetables.

Ratatouille is a dish that improves with a twenty-four-hour gestation, although I tend to make it in double quantities so I can serve it hot from the oven and then cold, as in this recipe, on a separate occasion. It's the perfect dish to have on standby for the weekend, as it goes with roast meats, cold cuts, kebabs, grilled meat and fish, with omelettes and scrambled egg. It's good, too, blanketed with grated cheese and popped under the grill.

1. Pre-heat the oven to 400F/200C/gas mark 6.

2. Keep the finished vegetables in separate piles. Peel, quarter and thinly slice the onion. Peel the garlic and finely chop. Quarter the red pepper lengthways, remove the seeds and finely slice each quarter across its width. Trim the unpeeled aubergine and quarter lengthways; finely slice each quarter. Split the courgettes lengthways and slice thinly. Pour boiling water over the tomatoes, count to 20, drain them under cold running water then peel. Remove the core and cut each tomato into eight pieces.

3. Heat half the olive oil in a wok or large frying pan and lightly brown the onions – this will take about 10 minutes – adding the garlic after a couple of minutes. Remove to a spacious bowl. Add the red pepper and allow it to wilt slightly. Remove. Meanwhile, place the aubergine in a bowl and sprinkle over half the remaining olive oil. Use your hands to mix it thoroughly and add the aubergines to the pan. Cook for 5 minutes, stirring a couple of times. Remove. Using the last of the olive oil, repeat the smearing business with the courgettes and add them to the pan. Cook for 5 minutes. Finally, stir in the tomatoes and season generously with salt and pepper. Cook for 5 minutes. Mix everything together, then turn the whole lot into an earthenware (or similar) dish. Smooth the surface, lay the bay leaf and thyme over the top and cover with aluminium foil. Bake for 35 minutes.

4. Spoon a mound of ratatouille into the middle of four serving plates.

5. Bring a small pan of water to the boil; add the vinegar. Crack an egg into a cup and carefully slip the egg into the pan. Once coagulated, add the second egg, and third and fourth. Keep the water at a gentle roll and cook for 2 minutes. Remove one egg at a time with a slotted spoon. Place an egg on top of a ratatouille pile, splash with olive oil and sprinkle with chives. Eat hot or cold.

Borani with Rocket and Shallot Salad

Serves 4 as a main course, 8 as a starter

Preparation: 15 minutes.
Cooking: 1 hour 25 minutes

400g onions
1 red pepper
2 tbsp vegetable oil
4 large garlic cloves
2 heaped tsp paprika
600g ripe tomatoes
200g round-grain rice
1 tsp salt
1 tsp fresh black pepper
3 tbsp chopped flat-leaf
    parsley

½ tbsp thyme leaves
1 tbsp finely chopped mint
2 tbsp olive oil
juice of ½ lemon
a little extra oil

For the salad:

150g rocket
2 shallots
½ tbsp balsamic vinegar
    mixed with 2 tbsp olive oil

While leafing through *The Melting Pot – Balkan Food and Cookery* by Maria Kaneva-Johnson, I came across Borani: Tomatoes with Rice. At the time I was looking for something to do with a mound of tomatoes which had passed their best; here, I found the answer.

Borani is an ancient Persian dish that has been through many changes. Recent versions are likely to be rice cooked with spinach, sauerkraut or tomatoes, which ends up as a sort of rice cake that can be sliced like a terrine.

I was so taken by the sound of borani that I cooked it immediately and, although I didn't have all the right ingredients, my slightly modified version turned out well, so I'd like to pass it on.

It's a wonderfully versatile dish which makes an excellent

starter with some sprigs of flat-leaf parsley and black olives, but is interesting and filling enough to be served as a main dish.

Try not to eat it immediately you take it out of the oven. It is better to let it settle in the dish for a little while before you turn it out. Refrigerate any leftovers, because it is delicious cold.

1. Peel and finely chop the onions. Core, de-seed and dice the pepper. Peel and finely chop the garlic. Peel, core, de-seed and chop the tomatoes. Wash the rice and drain.

2. Place the chopped onion and pepper in a heavy-based pan with the 2 tablespoons of vegetable oil. Cover and leave to cook slowly, stirring a couple of times, until the onions are softened but not browned. Allow about 10 minutes for this.

Stir in the garlic and paprika, cook for a couple of minutes and then add the tomatoes and leave, uncovered, to cook for 5 minutes. Add the rice and 250ml water, cover and cook on the lowest possible heat for about 35 minutes until all the liquid is absorbed, the mixture is thick and the rice tender.

Stir in the salt, pepper, herbs, 2 tablespoons of olive oil and lemon juice and taste for seasoning.

Transfer the mixture to a lightly oiled non-stick 10cm-square cake tin and smooth the top. Cut a piece of baking paper to fit exactly and bake in an oven pre-heated to 375F/190C/gas mark 5 for 20 minutes.

Remove the paper and cook for a further 15 minutes. Leave to cool for 10 minutes, run a knife round the lip, cover with a plate and quickly invert. Leave to cool and firm up before slicing.

3. To make the salad, wash and drain the rocket, finely dice the shallots and toss with the dressing.

Brown Tom

Serves 4　　　　　*Preparation: 20 minutes. Cooking: 35 minutes*

1kg ripe, full-flavoured
　tomatoes
150g brown wholemeal bread
　without crust
2 medium onions
1 very large garlic clove
25ml finely chopped flat leaf
　parsley

30ml finely chopped basil
6 tbsp freshly grated
　Parmesan
4 tbsp olive oil
25g butter
salt and freshly milled black
　pepper
extra Parmesan

Brown bread and tomatoes are the key ingredients in this surprisingly elegant summer gratin. It's simplicity itself to make, but does rely on using the best ingredients – decent wholemeal bread and tomatoes, 'grown for flavour' or 'sun-ripened on the vine'.

The bread is crumbed and mixed with very finely chopped onion, plenty of freshly chopped parsley and basil, and further seasoned with a mound of Parmesan. This is then piled into a well-oiled metal baking dish – I used one with a 25cm diameter and 5cm depth, but a square cake tin would be perfect – and layered with peeled and sliced tomatoes.

Each layer is seasoned generously with salt and pepper and a dribble of olive oil, and the top layer of bread is also covered with thin slices of butter.

While Brown Tom cooks in the oven, which it does at a high temperature, the most delectable smells permeate the house. The finished dish is indescribably good – the butter and olive oil mingle with the softened tomatoes and all these juices and flavours run into the bread, making it succulent and intensely flavoured.

This is a lovely dish to serve on its own for lunch or a lightish supper, and is well matched with simply cooked runner beans or minted peas and perhaps a few new potatoes. It would also be just the thing to serve with lamb.

There are a few important points about making Brown Tom: *don't* save time by not peeling the tomatoes – the rings of skin will spoil the texture; cut the onions *very* finely; *do* use a metal dish.

1. Place the tomatoes in a bowl and cover with boiling water. Count to twenty, drain in a colander and hold under the cold tap for a few seconds. Use a small sharp knife to remove the core and peel the tomatoes. Slice in thick rounds.

2. Chunk the bread and process to crumbs in a food processor.

3. Peel, halve and chop the onion very finely. Peel and finely chop the garlic. Mix together the breadcrumbs, onion, garlic, herbs and Parmesan and season with salt and pepper.

4. Use 1 tablespoon of the olive oil to grease a 25½cm diameter ×5cm metal oven dish (or something similar that holds 2 litres). Cover the bottom of the dish with one-third of the bread mixture and top with half the tomatoes laid out evenly. Season generously with salt and pepper and dribble over 1 tablespoon of the olive oil. Cover the tomatoes with another third of the bread mixture and then with the remaining tomatoes. Season with salt and pepper and another 1 tablespoon of olive oil. Finish with the remaining one third of bread mixture and dribble over the remaining olive oil. Finally, cover the bread with thin slices of butter.

5. Pre-heat the oven to 400F/200C/gas mark 6. Cook Brown Tom for 35 minutes in the middle of the hot oven until the top is well-browned and slightly crusty.

Serve from the dish, cut like a cake using a fish slice. Dust with more Parmesan.

Caserecce with Spinach, Roast Tomatoes and Goats Cheese

Serves 4   *Preparation: 20 minutes. Cooking: 35 minutes*

8 plum tomatoes
2 tbsp olive oil
½ tsp sugar
500g caserecce
400g spinach
125g mascarpone

200g goats cheese
1 small bird's eye chilli
juice of small lemon
salt and freshly milled black
    pepper

Caserecce is my new favourite pasta. Like all the best pasta it is made with durum wheat and is about the same length as penne, but it resembles a curled pleat, if you can imagine such a thing.

Anyway, it cooks swiftly and is the perfect pasta for this simple but quite delicious dish.

I used a big bag of fresh spinach to make the 'sauce' – a misnomer because all you do is blanch the spinach in boiling water, drain it carefully and give it a bit of a chop, then stir it into hot pasta, which has already been lubricated with mascarpone.

Also flavouring the caserecce is some very finely chopped bird's eye chilli, the tiny, slim and fiery red chilli stocked by most supermarkets, salt and lots of freshly grated black pepper, diced goats cheese, the juice of a small lemon and some roast tomatoes.

Roast tomatoes are wonderful to use in all manner of dishes. This way of cooking them will transform even the most anaemic tomatoes and give them a superb intensity of flavour.

The tomatoes have the skins slipped off – do bother with this – they are then halved, smeared with olive oil and seasoned with salt, pepper and sugar, and roasted for 30 minutes. The halves are halved again and mixed into the pasta with some diced goats cheese.

This dish is no trouble to make and manages to be everything you want on a weekday night: food that is comforting yet interesting, creamy yet spicy, and fresh as well as filling.

1. Pre-heat the oven to 400F/200C/gas mark 6.

2. Place tomatoes in a bowl and cover with boiling water. Count to twenty, drain and remove their skins.

Halve the tomatoes lengthways; lay out on a shallow baking tray smeared with a little of the olive oil.

Smear the cut surface of the tomatoes with olive oil, season with salt, pepper and sugar and cook in the oven for 30 minutes. Remove from the oven and halve the halves.

3. Cook the pasta according to packet instructions, allowing about 15 – 20 minutes for this. Drain it and toss with any remaining olive oil, then mix in the mascarpone, stirring until it has dissolved. Keep warm.

4. Meanwhile, put a large pan of salted water on to boil. Wash and pick over the spinach, removing any yellowed leaves and tough stalks (young, small leaves do not need their stalks removed), and when the water is boiling, blanch the spinach for 30 seconds.

Tip into a colander and hold the spinach under cold running water for 30 seconds or so and then drain, squeezing out all the water with your hands. Chop roughly.

5. De-seed and very finely chop the chilli pepper. Dice the goats cheese.

6. Stir the spinach into the pasta, mixing well, then do the same with the chilli.

Season well with pepper. Finally, stir in the lemon juice and loosely toss with the goats cheese and tomatoes. Eat.

Creole Sauce with Soft-Boiled Eggs and Herb Rice

Serves 4 *Preparation: 30 minutes. Cooking: 45 minutes*

3 tbsp vegetable oil

3 large onions

bunch spring onions

700g ripe tomatoes

2 branches fresh thyme

3 plump garlic cloves

2 tbsp grated fresh ginger

2 heaped tbsp chopped
   coriander leaves

1 heaped tbsp chopped
   flat-leaf parsley leaves

2 red peppers and 1 red chilli

salt and freshly milled black
   pepper

4 large, fresh eggs

For the herb rice:

225g basmati rice

2 tbsp chopped flat-leaf
   parsley leaves

1 tbsp finely snipped chives

2 spring onions

knob of butter

This sauce is the backbone of Mauritian cooking. It's dished up with rice, comes with kebabs and is spooned over grilled meat and fish from the barbecue. What makes it special is that the onions are cooked until they're sweet and succulent before all the other ingredients are mixed in. Spring onions, added after the other onions are soft, add a different mild onion flavour but the sauce has a freshness from lightly cooked tomatoes and a spicy interest from fresh ginger, garlic and chillies. Like ratatouille, which it resembles, it's good hot or cold and its flavours improve if made in advance.

You'll find creole sauce on the menu at Jason's (opposite 60 Blomfield Road, W9, 0171 286 6752) and Chez Liline (101 Stroud Green Road, N4, 0171 263 6550). There is much to discover on a Mauritian menu. This little-known cuisine is a cultural melting-pot born out of a mix that incorporates foods, flavours and cooking techniques from Portugal, Holland, France, India and China, all interwoven with influences from Creoles of mixed descent and the rich provender this island offers.

Creole sauce is a hybrid that could have been custom-designed to eat with chunky pasta, and it's always welcome chilled from the fridge and spooned into piping-hot baked potatoes.

1. Peel, halve and slice the onions. Gently heat the oil in a spacious pan. Stir in the onions, season with salt and pepper and cover.

Cook over a gentle heat, stirring a couple of times, for 30 minutes or until quite tender.

2. While the onions are cooking, trim and slice the spring onions. Cover the tomatoes with boiling water, count to twenty, drain and then peel and core them. Cut each tomato into six pieces. Peel the garlic cloves, chop and then crush them to a paste with ½ teaspoon of salt. Trim, de-seed and slice the red pepper. Finely chop the chilli. Add the spring onions, red pepper and chilli to the pan. Raise the heat slightly to cook off any liquid, and stir in the ginger, garlic, thyme, parsley and half the coriander. Cook briskly for 3 minutes. Add the tomatoes and cook for a further 5 minutes, stirring constantly. Garnish with the reserved coriander.

3. Cook the rice according to your favourite method. Stir in the parsley, chives, trimmed and sliced spring onions and butter. Meanwhile, bring a small pan of water to the boil. Spoon in the eggs and cook for 5 minutes. Drain, crack and peel immediately under cold running water.

For each serving, spoon some sauce over a mound of rice with the egg on top.

Eggs Masala and Poppadams

Serves 4　　　　　　*Preparation: 15 minutes. Cooking: 35 minutes*

4 garlic cloves
2½cm piece fresh ginger
2 cardamom pods
1 tsp coriander seeds
1 tsp cumin seeds
½ tsp whole cloves
½ tsp black peppercorns
½ tsp cayenne pepper

2 Spanish onions
2 tbsp vegetable oil
500g ripe tomatoes
2 tbsp fresh coriander leaves
6–8 fresh, free-range eggs
salt
lemon juice

One of my oldest friends and favourite dining companions comes from Singapore. He's possibly the greediest person I know. He always knows where to get the best char sui and freshest dim sum.

When not eating out, which he does almost every day, Lim is at home cooking. He's a fabulous cook, one of those naturals with an instinctive flair and unquenchable curiosity where food is concerned. His larder is full of interesting things and he's incredibly knowledgeable about the oddest ingredients. Take poppadams. His favourite brand is kept below the counter at an obscure Indian grocery in Earl's Court. He cooks them in the minimum of oil – just 1cm – for 2–3 seconds a side. He then stacks them like toast on several layers of absorbent kitchen paper laid out in a baking tray and leaves them in a very, very low oven for at least 1 hour, preferably overnight. By morning the paper is drenched with oil and the poppadams crisp and dry.

I make poppadams at the drop of a hat and particularly like using them to scoop up cold left-over curry and dal. They're almost essential with this recipe where the textures are soft and the spicy tomato and onion goo eminently scoopable.

The eggs should be the freshest and best you can lay your hands on. Look out for Martin Pitt's. His are date-stamped and produced on a 420-acre environmentally friendly farm.

1. Peel and chop the garlic. Peel and grate the ginger. Remove the seeds from the cardamom pods. Grind the cardamom, coriander, cumin, cloves and black peppercorns to a powder (an electric coffee grinder is ideal for this) and then add the garlic and ginger. Blitz to make a stiff masala paste and stir in the cayenne pepper.
2. Pour boiling water over the tomatoes, count to twenty and drain them. Remove the core and peel, then roughly chop the tomatoes.
3. Peel and finely dice the onions. Heat the oil in a wok or large saucepan over a medium-high heat and fry the onions until they turn caramel brown, stirring constantly so they brown evenly. This will take about 20 minutes.
4. Stir the masala paste into the onions and stir-fry for a couple of minutes. Add the tomatoes and a generous pinch of salt. Simmer vigorously for 10−15 minutes until the sauce begins to thicken. Taste and adjust the seasoning with more salt and lemon juice. If the tomatoes weren't ripe enough you may need to add a little sugar and a slug of ketchup.
5. Place the eggs in a pan, cover with water and bring to the boil. Cook for 10 minutes. Drain under running water, crack the eggs and remove their shells. Halve the eggs lengthways.
6. Get the sauce very hot, stir in most of the coriander and place the eggs in the sauce. Continue simmering until the eggs are warmed through. Sprinkle on the last of the coriander and serve with basmati rice, creamy natural yoghurt and chutneys. And poppadams.

Flamiche

Serves 4–6   *Preparation: 30 minutes. Cooking: 25 minutes*

900g leeks
75g butter
5–6 tbsp double cream
450g puff pastry or 2 × 250g
 ready-rolled puff pastry
 circles

1 beaten egg yolk with a
 splash of milk
a little flour
extra butter
salt and freshly milled black
 pepper

Flamiche is a Belgian leek tart – and also the name of a Michelin-starred restaurant about 80 miles north of Paris. I've never seen a restaurant decorated with leek-phernalia before (a beautiful cast-iron menu stand, table lamps etc.), and it's a great shame that there wasn't a single leek on the menu (leeks aren't as ubiquitous out of season in French supermarkets as they are in ours) when we made a detour to sample their namesake.

The rented house that Simon Hopkinson and I were staying at to work on our next book turned out to be stuffed full of magazines.

And it was while leafing through one of them, an out-of-date French food periodical, that Simon came across a full-colour photograph of the most gorgeous-looking leek tart either of us had ever seen. And, guess what? The recipe came from La Flamiche.

Needless to say, we both decided to have a go at cooking it back home (where, ironically, French leeks were on sale). If you follow Simon's cookery column in the *Independent* magazine on Saturday, you may already have cut out this recipe: he beat me to it.

It's the sort of pie that is good enough to eat on its own. It's also good with a tomato salad, but is a spectacular accompaniment to poached gammon. Come to think of it, bacon or ham of any sort would be good.

1. Trim leeks, cutting away most of the dark green (excellent for the stock pot), slice in thick rounds, wash carefully and drain thoroughly.

2. Melt the butter in a large frying pan and cook the leeks very gently for about 20 minutes until really soft. Season with salt and pepper, turn up the heat, and add the cream. Allow to bubble vigorously for a minute or two until the mixture is thick and creamy but not too wet. Tip on to a plate to cool.

3. Pre-heat the oven to 425F/220C/gas mark 7.

4. Halve the pastry, sprinkle a work surface with flour and roll the pastry into two identical circles. Place a baking tray in the oven. Smear a second flat baking tray with butter and cover with one of the puff-pastry circles. Spoon the cooled leeks on to the pastry, spreading them out to within 2½cm of the edge. Paint the border with beaten egg yolk.

5. Use the second pastry circle to form a lid and gently press the edges together all the way round. Brush the whole surface with egg wash and go round the border again, this time with the tines of a fork, pressing firmly. Make small slits in the centre of the flamiche to allow steam to escape and, if you wish, decorate with the point of a knife.

6. Slide the pie into the oven on to the pre-heated baking tray (this ensures a crisp, evenly cooked base). Bake for 25 minutes or until puffed, golden and spectacular. Cool for a few minutes before serving in wedges.

Gratin of Courgettes and Rice with Roast Beef Tomatoes

Serves 3–4   *Preparation: 20 minutes. Cooking: 20 minutes*

225g basmati rice

For the béchamel:
1 small onion
700ml milk
bay leaf
3 whole cloves
6 black peppercorns
2 sprigs fresh thyme
generous pinch salt
40g butter

3 tbsp flour
freshly grated nutmeg
6 heaped tbsp Parmesan
  cheese
500g courgettes
large knob of butter
4 beef tomatoes
small knob of butter
salt and freshly milled black
  pepper

In 'Letting Well Alone' in *An Omelette and a Glass of Wine*, Elizabeth David described a meal she'd eaten in a village inn near Aix-en-Provence. She keeps her descriptive prose on a tight rein but leaves you in no doubt that this is the best sort of genuine Provençal cooking that is both seasonal and freshly made, simple but traditional, and offered with the minimum of fuss.

No recipe is given for the gratin and I have to admit that I did tinker slightly with the bald description of courgettes cooked in butter, then sieved and mixed with béchamel (white sauce) and cooked rice.

As the original would have been made with full-fat, unpasteurized milk and butter, I added some Parmesan cheese by way of compensation. I also made a highly seasoned béchamel and served the dish risotto-style. This seemingly unpromising combination was both subtle and moreish and so good that I made it again the next day.

1. Cook the basmati rice your favourite way – I favour the absorption method when (well-washed) rice goes in a pan with sufficient water to cover. Allow to boil then immediately turn down the heat and clamp on a lid. Leave undisturbed to steam/simmer for around 15 minutes until all the water is absorbed and the grains tender and separate.

2. While the rice is cooking, make the béchamel. Chop the onion and place it in a pan with the milk, bay leaf, cloves, peppercorns, thyme and salt. Bring to the boil and simmer gently for 10 minutes. Remove from the heat, cover and leave for the time being.

3. Pre-heat the oven to 400F/200C/gas mark 6.

4. Trim, rinse, then grate the courgettes. Melt half the big knob of butter in a saucepan and stir in the grated courgettes. Season with salt and pepper, cover and leave to sweat gently, stirring a couple of times, for 2 minutes. Pour into a sieve to drain.

5. Finish the béchamel by melting 40g butter in a pan, stir in the flour, then strain over the milk, whisking as it boils to remove any lumps. Simmer gently for a few minutes.

6. Mix together the rice, béchamel and courgettes. Season with grated Parmesan and spoon the mixture into a buttered, shallow gratin dish. Smooth the top, dot with any remaining butter and sprinkle over the last of the Parmesan. Season with grated nutmeg.

7. Smear the tomatoes with a little butter and season. Place in a small baking dish.

8. Cook the gratin and tomatoes in the hot oven for 20 minutes until the gratin is nicely crusty and the tomatoes are blistered and puffy.

Leeks Vinaigrette with Yellow Tomatoes and Parmesan

Serves 6   *Preparation: 15 minutes. Cooking: 10 minutes*

1.8kg leeks

6 yellow tomatoes

Parmesan cheese

1 tbsp snipped chives or finely
   chopped parsley

For the vinaigrette:

pinch caster sugar

generous pinch salt

2 tbsp red wine vinegar

2 tbsp smooth Dijon mustard

1 large garlic clove

freshly milled black pepper

275ml vegetable oil or half
   olive oil

4 tbsp cold water

This is a new way of doing a classic dish and is a radical improvement. Instead of pouring vinaigrette over whole cooked leeks, cut the leeks lengthways in halves or quarters, depending on their thickness, and slice them into 7½cm–10cm chunks. This way the dressing can really get in between the layers of leek, served in manageable-sized pieces.

You don't actually need any embellishment with leeks vinaigrette, but it becomes even better when matched with a soft poached egg or has a hard-boiled egg grated over the top. Tomatoes, too, go very well with leeks, as does Parmesan cheese, either grated or flaked, as in this recipe.

1. Trim the leeks, removing the tough dark-green ends and any blemished outer leaves, and leave to soak in cold water.

2. While the leeks are soaking, make the vinaigrette. Stir the sugar and salt into the vinegar and pour into the bowl of a food processor with the mustard, garlic (peeled), and pepper. Blitz at high speed then add the oil in a gradual stream, followed by the water to give the vinaigrette a pale, glossy emulsion and creamy texture. Leftovers, and there will be some, can be kept in a jar in the fridge for a couple of weeks.

3. Drain the leeks and put a large pan of water on to boil. Add 1 teaspoon of salt and fling in the leeks. Cook at a vigorous boil, testing for tenderness with the point of a small knife after 4 minutes. Drain carefully – thin leeks will flop about – squeezing out excess water. I prefer to use a steamer to avoid this water-logging (the same timing applies; the leeks added once the water boils) but the downside is that their colour fades. Anyway, cool the leeks slightly, then split lengthways into halves or quarters, depending on their thickness, and cut into 7½cm–10cm sections. Lay them out on a serving dish, cut side uppermost, and spoon over a good amount of vinaigrette.

4. Place the tomatoes in a bowl, cover with boiling water and count to fifteen (twenty if using red tomatoes). Drain and peel the tomatoes, using a small sharp knife to nip out their cores. Cut into thick slices and arrange over the leeks. Sprinkle with the herbs. Next, use a potato peeler to cut shavings of Parmesan and cover the tomatoes generously. If you serve this with a soft-boiled egg per person, it becomes a light meal with plenty of crusty bread and butter.

Mushroom Lasagne
with Parsley

Serves 4–6   *Preparation: 40 minutes. Cooking: 1 hour 15 minutes*

40g dried porcini
500g large, flat black
  mushrooms
225g brown chestnut
  mushrooms
juice of 1 lemon
4 garlic cloves
2 tbsp olive oil

For the béchamel:
1 medium onion
2 cloves
1 bay leaf

4 black peppercorns
¼ tsp salt
500ml milk
65g butter
2 flat tbsp flour
50ml single cream
salt and fresh black pepper
bunch of flat-leaf parsley
6 sheets dried egg lasagne
1 tbsp chopped fresh sage
freshly grated nutmeg
2 tbsp freshly grated Parmesan

This recipe is very loosely based on Vincisgrassi Maceratese, a nineteenth-century lasagne re-created by Franco Taruschio for his menu at the Walnut Tree near Abergavenny. Franco makes his own silky-thin lasagne and sandwiches it with locally collected porcini, adding scraps of prosciutto or Parma ham, and bathes the layers in a luxurious béchamel sauce. His version is quite simply one of the best things I've ever eaten. However, this vegetarian version is pretty good too.

What gives the dish its intensely mushroomy flavour and satisfying meaty texture is the high proportion of mushrooms; pre-cooking them reduces their volume and concentrates the mushroom flavour. And when layered up with a highly seasoned and parsley-flavoured béchamel sauce, the whole covered generously with Parmesan, the combination of textures and flavours is beyond compare.

This dish could be prepared in advance and then popped into the oven for about thirty minutes.

1. Cover the porcini with boiling water and leave for 20 minutes. Drain.

2. Slice the flat black mushrooms. Rinse the whole chestnut mushrooms. Peel and finely chop the garlic. Place all the mushrooms and the garlic in a roasting tray and dribble over the olive oil and lemon juice. Mix everything together and season with salt and black pepper. Bake in a hot oven (400F/200C/gas mark 6) for 30 minutes until the mushrooms are thoroughly cooked.

3. Meanwhile peel and roughly chop the onion and place it in a pan with the cloves, bay leaf, peppercorns, salt and milk. Bring to the boil, simmer for 10 minutes, cover and turn off the heat. Leave for 30 minutes. Melt the butter in a separate pan, stir in the flour and beat in the strained milk to make a thick roux. Simmer for 10 minutes and add the cream. Blanch the parsley leaves in boiling water, chop finely and add to the sauce. Taste and adjust the seasoning.

4. Cook the lasagne in plenty of boiling salted water for 15 minutes. Drain and dry on a tea towel.

5. Take a shallow rectangular dish that can fit two sheets of lasagne and cover with some of the béchamel. Put in a layer of lasagne and top with a thin layer of béchamel. Cover with half the drained mushrooms, sprinkle with salt and sage and repeat, ending with a thick layer of béchamel. Dust with nutmeg and then with Parmesan and bake in a hot oven (400F/200C/gas mark 6) for 35 minutes.

Parsley Potato Gnocchi with Sage Butter and Parmesan

Serves 4   *Preparation: 30 minutes. Cooking: 20 minutes*

900g floury potatoes
350g flour
2 tbsp finely chopped flat-leaf
    parsley
1 tbsp finely snipped chives
Salt, freshly grated black
    pepper and nutmeg

3 tbsp freshly grated
    Parmesan
3 large egg yolks
75g butter
6 sage leaves
extra Parmesan

The Henry Doubleday Research Association at Ryton Organic Gardens in Warwickshire once invited me to give a cookery demonstration at their annual Potato Day. One of the dishes I chose was these little potato dumplings made with mashed potato, flour and egg. Gnocchi are very simple to make and so much better than the rubbery ready-made version sold in unappetizing plastic bags by grocers and supermarkets.

Home-made gnocchi is child's play. Mashed potato – mashed, that is, without milk or butter – is mixed with less than half its weight in flour and made light and elastic with egg yolks. The mixture is then worked into a dough, rolled into a long sausage, cut off into nuggets and quickly cooked in boiling water.

They are light and fluffy but substantial and are delicious with just a generous shower of freshly grated Parmesan. They also go very well with melted butter and are very good, too, either with a herby fresh tomato sauce or blanketed in creamy béchamel, particularly when the sauce is covered with Parmesan and flashed briefly under a hot grill until the surface is blistered and crusty.

These gnocchi are flavoured with herbs, nutmeg and Parmesan, and served with sage-flavoured butter. They go wonderfully well with baked tomatoes and a floppy green salad, dressed with a vinaigrette into which a dollop of mayonnaise or cream has been mixed.

1. Cook the peeled potatoes in plenty of salted boiling water and drain thoroughly. Mash carefully and transfer to a large mixing bowl. Sift over two-thirds of the flour, ½ teaspoon of salt, a generous seasoning of pepper and nutmeg, the herbs and three tablespoons of grated Parmesan.

2. Use your fingertips to work everything together; make a well in the middle and add the egg yolks to make a soft, sticky mixture. Dust a work surface with flour, then take a handful of the potato, dip it into the remaining flour, taking only sufficient to stiffen the mixture slightly and make it less sticky. Knead lightly and roll with the flat of your hand into a sausage the thickness of a fat finger. Cut off 2½cm lengths and transfer to a lightly floured baking sheet. Dust with flour. Continue in this way until all the potato mixture is used up.

3. Put a large pan of salted water on to boil. Meanwhile, melt the butter in a small pan with the sage leaves. Scoop off the white froth that forms and keep warm. Drop the gnocchi in the boiling water and cook in batches, letting the dumplings boil for 3 minutes once they pop up to the surface. Scoop out with a slotted spoon, drain the spoon on kitchen paper and transfer to a hot serving dish. Dribble over the butter, cover with a generous shower of Parmesan and serve immediately.

Potato Pithivier

Serves 6–8　　　　　*Preparation: 40 minutes. Cooking: 55 minutes*

600ml double cream or half
　double cream and half
　full-cream milk
1 bay leaf
2 branches fresh thyme
1kg boiling potatoes
2 garlic cloves

½ teaspoon grated nutmeg
350g ready-rolled puff pastry
knob of butter or 1 tbsp oil
salt and freshly milled black
　pepper
1 egg whisked with 2 tbsp milk

One of the time-honoured perks for a film crew working on a programme about food is that they get to eat the grub when shooting ends.

So it can be daunting indeed when they pounce on your nervous labours and start pontificating about how Delia, Gary or Rick, or some other favourite TV chef, does the dish you've just cooked.

It's pretty awful too, as happened to me when I cooked this potato pie on a recent programme, if something as mundane as salt gets forgotten.

Salt is vital to potatoes. And when they're cooked in cream, as they are in this luscious pie, you need plenty of it.

The best way of describing the pie is to call it pommes dauphinoise wrapped in pastry. In this version the sliced potatoes are almost entirely cooked in seasoned cream before being spooned into a puff-pastry case.

In order to make this pie look as regal as its rich flavours demand, I cooked it in a round tin and decorated the lid. I got the idea from the stylish-looking large round puff-pastry tarts that are a speciality of Pithiviers, in the Orléans region of France.

1. Place the cream or cream and milk in a large saucepan – later it will also hold the potatoes – with the bay leaf and thyme. Season with salt and black pepper. Set over a high heat and bring to the boil. Simmer for 10 minutes then turn off the heat and cover the pan.

2. Peel and slice the potatoes very thinly. Rinse and drain them. Peel and very finely chop the garlic. Bring the cream back to the boil and add the potatoes and garlic. Stir thoroughly and bring back to the boil. Cook for a couple of minutes.

3. Thinly roll out two-thirds of the pastry and use it to line a well-buttered/oiled 25½cm-diameter, 5cm-deep metal pie dish, leaving plenty drooping over the edge. Season again, adding the nutmeg. Roll out the remaining pastry and cut it to fit the top generously. Pour the potato and cream mixture into the pie crust and fold the edges over, nipping and tucking to prevent leakages. This is very important. Use a pastry brush to paint the pastry flaps with egg wash, then fit the lid into place. Paint the lid with the rest of the egg wash. Use a small sharp knife to etch a pattern into the pastry. I made a ring round the middle of the pie and curved triangles radiating out of a pin-prick hole at the pie's centre.

4. Pre-heat the oven to 500F/250C/gas mark 9 and place a pastry sheet in the middle. Put the pie on the hot pastry sheet and cook for 10 minutes. Lower the temperature to 325F/170C/gas mark 3 and bake for a further 45 minutes.

5. Remove the pie from the oven and run a knife around the inside edge of the dish. Cover it with a large plate and invert the pie. Repeat with a second plate. Eat hot, warm or cold. Perfect for a picnic.

Spanish Omelette with Gremolata and Parmesan

Serves 2 as a main course   Preparation: 20 minutes. Cooking: 30 minutes

3 tbsp olive oil
1 Spanish onion
300g potatoes, preferably a
    waxy variety
salt and freshly milled pepper
4 large, fresh eggs

Tabasco
bunch of flat-leaf parsley
2 plump garlic cloves
½ small lemon
Parmesan

This omelette – or Tortilla de Patatas to give it its real name – is dense with pre-cooked potato and onion and is cut like a cake and eaten in wedges. It can be eaten hot, warm or cold, features on tapas menus far and wide, and in Spain is a universal picnic staple.

You can of course, make this omelette in any frying pan, but I've found I get the best results when I use either a deep-sided non-stick pan or my trusty old Le Creuset. The important point here is to oil the (hot) pan thoroughly so that the omelette slips out without sticking. This is important only if you plan to make the tortilla in advance to eat warm or cold.

Gremolata or gremolada, as it's sometimes called, is a mixture of finely chopped parsley, garlic and lemon peel. It's an Italian garnish – without the lemon it becomes French persillade – which adds a fresh and fiery finish to fried and poached foods and goes very well with potatoes.

I think the omelette is particularly good eaten with tomatoes in some form or other. A quick tomato sauce (three chopped spring onions and one small garlic clove stewed in butter until tender and then boiled hard for 2–3 minutes with six peeled and chopped tomatoes and a slug of ketchup) would be ideal. A green salad would also be good.

1. Begin by preparing the gremolata which, together with the grated Parmesan cheese, is strewn over the top of the finished omelette. Use the flat of a knife to crack the garlics, flake away their skins and chop finely. Pick the leaves from the parsley and chop very finely; you should have about 2 tablespoons. Grate the lemon peel and chop small. Mix everything together. Have ready 2 tablespoons of freshly grated Parmesan cheese.

2. Place the potatoes in a pan, cover with water and bring to the boil. Add half a teaspoon of salt and cook for 10–15 minutes until tender to the point of a knife.

3. While the potatoes are cooking, peel and halve the onion and chop into small dice. Smear the inside edges of a 20½cm-diameter frying pan with a little of the olive oil. Heat the pan, and when it's smoking add the remaining oil. Let the oil run round the pan and then add the onion. Turn down the heat immediately, season the onion with salt and pepper and cook gently, stirring frequently, for about 10 minutes until the onion has softened.

4. Drain the potatoes under cold running water, pull away their skins and dice the flesh. Add them to the pan with the onion and stir-fry for a couple of minutes.

5. Pre-heat an overhead grill.

6. Whisk the eggs, and season with salt and pepper and a few drops of Tabasco. Turn up the heat under the vegetables and pour the egg into the pan. Cook for about 45 seconds or until the base of the omelette is uniformly thickened. Remove the pan to the grill and cook the top of the omelette until puffy and golden. Using an egg slice, ease the omelette out of the pan on to a large plate. Strew first with gremolata and then with Parmesan.

Spinach and Ricotta Parmesan Pie with Red Salad and Black Olives

Serves 4   *Preparation: 25 minutes. Cooking: 45 minutes*

6 spring onions
2 plump garlic cloves
6–8 tbsp olive oil
500g spinach
3 tbsp chopped dill fronds
1 tbsp finely chopped mint
2 tbsp pine kernels
225g ricotta cheese
3 eggs
a few drops of Tabasco
nutmeg
½ tsp salt and ½ tsp black
    pepper

150g filo pastry
3 tbsp freshly grated Parmesan

For the salad:
1 scant tbsp balsamic vinegar
pinch salt and of sugar
2 tbsp olive oil
1 red onion (around 125g)
3 large ripe plum tomatoes
    (around 350g)
12 black olives
2 tbsp roughly chopped
    flat-leaf parsley

I'd originally intended to make this recipe as an open tart, mixing grated Parmesan into regular shortcrust pastry. Instead, when time ran out, I reached for the fresh filo pastry lurking at the bottom of my fridge.

About half-way through making the pie with filo, I realized that I was more or less making Greek spanakopitta. That, too, involves spinach, onions and a mild cheese mixed with eggs wrapped in filo pastry, but this version also includes a hint of garlic and chilli and a strong flavour of fresh dill. I also sprinkled grated Parmesan between the layers of filo pastry and, by way of a texture contrast, added a few toasted pine kernels.

The crisp pastry and succulent filling goes well with this salad of red onions, tomatoes, flat-leaf parsley and black olives, but if you prefer a gentler taste some new potatoes would be perfect.

Incidentally, the pie is also good cold, and resilient enough for picnics.

1. Trim and finely slice the spring onions and garlic. Pick over the spinach, removing stalks and withered, nasty bits. Heat a small frying pan and stir-fry the pine kernels until evenly browned.
2. Heat 1 tablespoon of olive oil and soften the spring onions and garlic, then add the spinach in handfuls, adding more as it wilts. Stir in the dill and mint, and cook for 5 minutes in total until the spinach weeps copiously. Tip into a colander to drain; press down with your hand.
3. Whisk the eggs, add Tabasco, a good grating of nutmeg, salt and pepper and crumble in the ricotta and drained spinach.
4. Oil a shallow ceramic dish (around 20cm × 30cm) and cover it with overlapping sheets of double-thickness filo pastry. Paint the pastry with oil, sprinkle with some of the Parmesan and continue building double layers with plenty of overhang until two-thirds of the filo is used up. Pour in the filling, loosely fold over the overhang and continue the layering, tucking and folding to make a neat top. Paint the top generously with oil and score the top in squares or diagonals, taking care not to cut through to the filling. Bake at 375F/190C/gas mark 5 for 35 minutes. Turn off the oven and leave for 10 minutes (or longer) before serving.
5. Mix vinegar, salt, pepper and sugar in a salad bowl before stirring in the oil. Peel, halve and wafer-slice the onion. Quarter the tomatoes, remove pips and chunk. Stone the olives and roughly chop. Add parsley. Mix.

Spring Vegetables with Lemon Butter

Serves 2   *Preparation: 15 minutes. Cooking: 15 minutes*

350g small new potatoes
225g French beans
8 or more asparagus tips
1 tsp salt

For the lemon butter:
juice from 1 large lemon
2 tablespoons water
125g butter cut into small
    chunks
extra squeeze of lemon
bunch fresh chives

This recipe is a celebration of two favourite treats – Jersey Royal potatoes and English asparagus. Peeled new potatoes, asparagus spears and French beans are bathed in a pungent lemon butter that is laced with chives. It's a simple idea which could be adapted with different combinations of vegetables such as broad and runner beans and courgettes, and I think it makes a lovely light supper. Remember, too, to serve with simply cooked fish or chicken.

1. Scrape the potatoes, rinse thoroughly and place in a saucepan with enough water to cover. Bring to the boil, add ½ teaspoon of salt and cook for 10–15 minutes until tender to the point of a knife. Remove from the heat, drain and keep warm.

2. Place the lemon juice and water in a small pan and heat gently until slightly syrupy and reduced by about two-thirds. This will happen very quickly, so keep an eye on the pan. Lower the heat to a mere thread and whisk in the butter bit by bit until it is thoroughly amalgamated and the texture turns creamy. Season, adding a final squeeze of fresh lemon and serve warm.

3. Meanwhile, bring two large pans of water to the boil. Add ½ teaspoon salt to each, establish a vigorous boil and throw the beans into one pan and the asparagus in the other. Cook the beans for 2 minutes and the asparagus for 3. Drain, plunge quickly into cold water, but keep the vegetables separate and drain again. Place the beans in a serving dish with the potatoes. Snip the chives into the warm sauce and pour over the vegetables. Mix together so everything is coated with the sauce and then carefully mix in the asparagus. Delicious eaten with (more) salt and freshly milled black pepper and slabs of soda bread spread with decent butter.

Dishes for One or Two

Many of my recipes in the *Evening Standard* are for two, sometimes one, because that's how I reckon a large proportion of Londoners eat. Many of the dishes, such as Dijon chicken escalopes, and sesame broccoli stir-fry with chilli, garlic and rice noodles, are really no more than quick and simple ideas. Others, such as balsamic chicken, onion and garlic, and roast quail with sage potato sandwiches and quick French peas, sound complicated but are deceptively easy and speedy to make. Some dishes, such as sardines with rocket and tomato, are inspired by restaurant meals and would be impracticable to make at home for a lot of people.

Almost Carbonara

Serves 2–3   *Preparation: 10 minutes. Cooking: 15 minutes*

100g streaky bacon
1 tbsp olive oil
2 plump garlic cloves
2 eggs
1 egg yolk
2 tbsp whipping cream

175g penne rigate
salt and freshly milled black
    pepper
1 tbsp finely chopped flat-leaf
    parsley or chives (optional)
freshly grated Parmesan

Spaghetti alla carbonara, or Italian eggs and bacon as some people call it, is one of those seemingly simple dishes that are easy to get horribly wrong.

It doesn't involve many ingredients, but the two most important are fresh free-range eggs and decent streaky bacon. The idea is to cook the spaghetti al dente and then, at the last minute, to toss it with beaten raw egg and crisply cooked bacon.

The heat in the spaghetti must be sufficient to cook the egg very slightly so it coats and clings to the pasta with occasional soft grainy flecks.

If the eggs end up solid like scrambled eggs the whole point of the dish is lost.

Some people also add cream or cream and Parmesan to the equation. I like to include garlic and plenty of black pepper to introduce a fiery note.

Another personal preference is to make carbonara with a short stubby pasta such as penne or rigatoni instead of the more usual spaghetti.

This has the advantage of trapping the creamy egg around and inside the pasta tubes. It's also – and this will appeal to those whose fork technique leaves something to be desired – easier to eat than spaghetti.

All you may wish for with this is a salad of floppy green leaves to mop up any egg left at the bottom of the bowl. Crusty bread with decent butter and plenty of red wine would be good accompaniments.

1. Using a wooden spoon, beat the whole eggs, egg yolk and cream and season with salt and plenty of pepper.

2. Cook the penne according to packet instructions in plenty of boiling salted water with ½ tablespoon of olive oil.

3. Chop the bacon into thick matchsticks 10 minutes before the pasta is ready. Heat the rest of the olive oil in a frying pan and cook the bacon gently so it releases most of its fat before it crisps. Peel the garlic and chop very finely. Add it to the bacon, stirring so it browns evenly and doesn't burn, for the last 30 seconds of cooking.

4. When the pasta is ready, drain it thoroughly and mix immediately with the hot bacon and garlic, then pour in the egg and cream mixture. Stir to coat the pasta evenly and add the parsley/chives if using. Dust with Parmesan and serve immediately in hot bowls. Provide extra Parmesan.

A Luscious Quick Stew

Serves 2–3   *Preparation: 20 minutes. Cooking: 40 minutes*

2 tbsp cooking oil
3 rashers streaky bacon
1 large red onion, approx.
    250–300g
2 large field mushrooms
200g tender lean steak
1 bay leaf
1 heaped tbsp flour
1 wine glass red wine

1 wine glass stock (made with
    ½ stock cube) or water
1 scant tbsp redcurrant jelly
3 medium carrots
100g frozen peas
½ tbsp freshly chopped
    parsley
salt and freshly milled pepper

This is the perfect recipe for the times when you want the comfort of a good old-fashioned stew but haven't the time to make it properly, using one of the more appropriate cuts, such as chuck or shin, that need long, slow cooking.

This recipe could be made with any lean and tender piece of meat that can be cooked relatively quickly though inevitably that means a more expensive cut. The good news is that, because this stew is fortified with all manner of other ingredients, you need less meat than usual.

The meat is cut across the width into relatively thin slices and tossed in flour, which will thicken the stew. Extra flavour comes from a bay leaf, some diced streaky bacon, a large red onion, two big field mushrooms, gravy made with a glass of red wine and a little stock made with half a stock cube.

A spoonful of redcurrant jelly stirred into the stew adds a depth of flavour and slight sweetness that makes a terrific difference to the gravy. A few carrots are finely sliced – on the slant to make them look a bit special – and cooked separately and flung in along with some frozen peas right at the end of cooking.

The stew is served with a sprinkling of chopped parsley and needs a bowl of creamy mashed potato on the side.

1. Chop bacon into lardons. Peel and halve the onion, dice one half and slice the other. Trim the meat and slice it across the grain in thin diagonal strips. Place the meat in a bowl and toss with the flour.

2. Over a low–medium flame, heat half the oil in a heavy-bottomed pan. Cook the bacon until beginning to crisp then add the onion with the bay leaf.

After about five minutes, when it's starting to look juicy, add the sliced mushrooms and ½ teaspoon of salt and a generous seasoning of pepper. Stir so the mushrooms cook evenly and, after a few minutes, tip the contents of the pan on to a plate.

3. Lower the flame and heat the remaining oil in the pan. Add the meat and all the flour, stirring it. Cover the pan and leave for 2–3 minutes. Toss the meat and return the lid, making sure the meat is brown and the flour isn't sticking. Cook for a couple more minutes.

4. Remove the lid and add the wine, stirring to scrape up the bits off the bottom of the pan and make a thick gravy. Add the redcurrant jelly and, when it's dissolved, add the stock or water. Establish a gentle simmer then return the onion mixture and leave to cook very gently for about 15 minutes.

Meanwhile, trim and peel the carrots and slice thinly on the diagonal. Cook in a separate pan in a small amount of salted water for about 5 minutes until just tender. Add the carrots and peas to the stew, simmer for a few minutes, check the seasoning and serve sprinkled with parsley.

Aubergine Lasagne with Mint

Serves 2—3   *Preparation: 30 minutes. Cooking: 20 minutes*

500g medium-sized tomatoes
2 medium onions
2 plump garlic cloves
1 tbsp tomato ketchup
2 plump aubergines
4 tbsp olive oil

For the béchamel sauce:
425ml milk
1 small onion
1 garlic clove
1 bay leaf
6 black peppercorns

4 branches fresh thyme
40g butter
2 heaped tbsp flour
4 tbsp whipping cream
3 tbsp chopped flat-leaf
    parsley
1 tbsp chopped fresh mint
2 tbsp freshly grated
    Parmesan
salt and freshly milled black
    pepper

Aubergine has a curiously meaty texture, and when it's cut length-ways in slices it becomes a useful ingredient. For this dish I've precooked aubergine slices and used them like lasagne, layered with a fresh tomato sauce and thick béchamel, the whole inter-leaved with a generous seasoning of fresh parsley and mint.

The top is dredged with grated Parmesan and the dish is cooked briefly in the oven, just long enough to heat everything through but not let it merge into a gooey mess.

The aubergines are best pre-cooked on a ridged cast-iron grill pan, but a heavy-based frying pan will do almost as well, and they could be cooked in the oven. It is important the slices are cooked through completely at this stage.

This is a rich and satisfying dish that requires no other side dish. A green salad served afterwards would be just the thing.

1. Pour boiling water over the tomatoes, count to twenty, tip into a colander and hold under cold running water. Use a small sharp knife to nick out the cores and roughly chop. Peel the onions and chop. Crush and peel the garlic and chop. Place all these ingredients in a pan with the tomato ketchup and a seasoning of salt and pepper and cook at a vigorous simmer until thick and jam-like. This takes about 15 minutes.

2. Next the béchamel: peel and chop the onion, crack the garlic with your fist and place in a pan with the milk, peppercorns, cloves, bay leaf, thyme and a pinch of salt. Bring slowly to the boil, simmer for 5 minutes, then cover and turn off the heat. Leave for at least 10 minutes. Melt the butter in a pan, stir in the flour and, when amalgamated, pour the milk through a sieve into the pan, whisking as it comes to the boil. Simmer gently for 5 minutes, stir in the cream and cook for a further 5 minutes.

3. Meanwhile, wash and trim the aubergines. Cut lengthways into 5cm slices and place in a large bowl. Sprinkle over the olive oil, working quickly to smear the slices all over with oil. Don't be mingy about this but, equally, don't drench them. Heat a cast-iron grill pan or heavy frying pan over a medium heat, lay out the slices, turning them after about 3 minutes, and repeat on the other side; you want them tender but not over-cooked.

4. Smear a shallow ovenproof dish with olive oil and spread 2 tablespoons of the béchamel across the base. Repeat with the tomato and cover with slices of aubergine. Season with salt, pepper and one-third of the herbs. Repeat this process twice, but being more generous with the tomato and béchamel, making sure you've reserved enough béchamel to cover the top. Sprinkle over the grated Parmesan and cook in a hot oven (400F/200C/gas mark 6) for 15–20 minutes until the top is crusty.

Balsamic Chicken, Onion and Garlic

Serves 2   *Preparation: 15 minutes. Cooking: 30 minutes*

2 large onions
25g butter
1 tbsp vegetable oil
2 plump garlic cloves
4 chicken thighs or 2 chicken
    breasts

2 tbsp balsamic vinegar
4 tbsp chicken stock or water
salt and freshly milled black
    pepper

It's incredible the effect a generous slug of balsamic vinegar has on a simple chicken dish such as this, turning it into something rather special.

This is hardly surprising when you consider that aceto balsamico is no ordinary vinegar. It has been made in Modena for centuries, and even the cheaper (sic) brands are made by maturing the juice of (mainly) Trebbiano grapes for several years in various different woods and barrels gradually diminishing in size.

It's the maturing that develops the flavour (and price) of this soy sauce lookalike, and the older the vinegar the higher the price tag. It's a fact that the more you pay, the better the balsamico, but even the cheapest little bottle will impart an extraordinarily deep, mild and slightly sweet flavour, and spicy aroma to your cooking.

Use it sparingly, regarding it as a seasoning, to transform vinaigrettes, stews and casseroles, and notice the difference it makes when you use it to deglaze pans. Try a few drops over grilled meat and vegetables.

More eccentrically, it is delicious sprinkled over hulled strawberries and ripe, honeyed pears.

In this dish, the chicken, onions and garlic are all effectively cooked before the balsamico is added. Don't be alarmed that the vinegar is allowed almost entirely to bubble away; it will leave behind a haunting flavour and deep, dark reddish-brown colour. This is a moist, rather than sauced, dish that is nicely accompanied by buttery mashed potato and plainly boiled green vegetables such as broccoli or lightly cooked thick batons of courgette.

1. Peel and halve the onions. Rather than slice in the usual way across the onion, cut into chunky half moons. Peel the garlic and slice in wafer-thin rounds — the centre will probably fall out (this is the new growth beginning to sprout).

2. If using chicken thighs, remove the skin and cut the flesh off the bones in big chunks and slice it into bite-sized pieces. If using breast, remove the skin and slice as before.

3. Heat the butter and oil in a frying pan over a medium flame and when the butter is bubbling add the onions. Toss them around allowing to colour and brown in patches. After 10 minutes add the garlic; continue stir-frying, adjusting the heat so everything cooks briskly and colours evenly without burning. Season with salt and pepper, cook for a further 5–10 minutes until the onion is more or less tender and add the chicken. Continue stir-frying until all the chicken has turned from pink to white.

4. Now add the vinegar and, after a few seconds, when it has bubbled up, coloured the chicken and almost entirely disappeared, add the stock or water.

Lower the heat and leave to simmer very gently, stirring everything around every so often, for about 10 minutes. Adjust seasoning and serve.

Crisp Chicken Wings with Avocado Salsa

Serves 2 *Preparation: 25 minutes plus 30 minutes marinading.*
Cooking: 25 minutes

750g chicken wings, fins
    trimmed (perfect for the
    stock pot)
4 tbsp olive oil
juice of 1 lemon
1 tbsp balsamic vinegar
1 garlic clove crushed to a
    paste with a generous
    pinch of salt
1 tsp thyme leaves

For the salsa:
1 slightly under-ripe avocado
4 spring onions
4 plum tomatoes
a handful of coarsely chopped
    coriander leaves
juice of ½ lemon
1 tbsp olive oil
4 drops Tabasco
salt and freshly milled black
    pepper

Ever one for a bargain, I couldn't resist the chicken wings on sale at my butcher's. He tends to sell them for the stock pot although they're regarded as a delicacy in Chinese kitchens.

There isn't, of course, much meat on these little bones but if you buy plenty of them and treat them right they make a delicious, hands-on supper.

They need to be marinated for at least 30 minutes, preferably an hour, then roasted fast and hot so the skin crisps up over the moist meat. This is definitely food to eat with your fingers.

The salsa is almost a meal in itself and the soft, creamy avocado and tart lemon and coriander dressing goes well with the chicken. Leftovers would work well in toasted pitta envelopes.

Crusty bread would be a good accompaniment.

1. Mix together the olive oil, lemon juice, balsamic vinegar, garlic and thyme in a bowl that can hold all the chicken wings. Slash the wings in several places with a small sharp knife and using your hands smear them around in the marinade until all the pieces are coated. Leave for at least 30 minutes.

2. Heat the oven to 400F/200C/gas mark 6. Set a wire rack over a baking tray and cover with the chicken wings. Cook in the hot oven for 10 minutes, then turn down the heat to 325F/170C/gas mark 3. Leave for 15–20 minutes until the wings are golden.

3. Make the salsa 5 minutes before the wings are ready by stirring a generous pinch of salt and pepper into the lemon juice, then whisking in the Tabasco and olive oil. Peel and dice the avocado. Core, seed and finely chop the tomatoes. Trim and finely slice the spring onions, discarding the dark green section. Tip everything into the dressing, mix in the chopped coriander.

Pile the wings into a bowl, sprinkle with salt and eat very hot while forking up mouthfuls of the salsa.

Dijon Chicken Escalopes

Serves 2   *Preparation: 10 minutes. Cooking: 10 minutes*

2 skinned chicken breasts   15g butter
2 slices wholemeal bread   1 tbsp cooking oil
2 tbsp smooth Dijon mustard   lemon wedges to serve
1 egg   2 sheets greaseproof paper
flour for dusting
salt and freshly milled black
    pepper

Here's a wizard wheeze for a delicious and quick supper made
with chicken breasts. The breast is placed between two sheets of
greaseproof paper and bashed firmly several times with a rolling
pin or meat cleaver, if you have such a thing, until flattened to
almost double its size.

You have to be a bit careful doing this, because you don't want
to smash the meat to smithereens, but on the other hand you
need to be quite aggressive to have any effect.

The meat is now dipped in flour and one side is spread with
Dijon mustard. It's then seasoned with salt and plenty of freshly
milled black pepper, dipped in beaten egg and then in wholemeal
breadcrumbs.

Next, a little butter and cooking oil is heated in a frying pan
and the escalopes are fried over a moderate heat until crisp and
golden. If you prefer, you could cut the beaten breast into strips,
then follow the same procedure to make goujons of Dijon chicken.

These are the perfect TV snack – because you make a great
pile (keeping them warm on a wire tray over an oven dish in a
low oven while you make more) – along with a creamy dipping

sauce or a smear of the new Hellmann's mustard mayonnaise.

Another good idea is to pile the goujons into thick slices of mayo-buttered, very fresh wholemeal bread. These tender, crisp-shelled escalopes with their hidden flavour will go with any potato dish – the plainer the better. Having said that, and it probably sounds peculiar, I squeezed fresh lemon juice into mashed potato to serve with mine.

This was delicious and a perfect accompaniment, being both creamy and soft with a hint of fresh citrus. In fact, you will be squeezing lemon juice over the escalopes and some is bound to get in with the mash, so it's not as odd as it seems.

1. Lay out the chicken breasts with plenty of space between and around them on a sheet of greaseproof paper. Cover with the second piece of paper and gently bash the meat until flattened and about half as big again. Smear one side of each escalope with mustard. Season with salt and pepper.

2. Remove the crusts from the bread, tear into pieces and blitz in the food processor to make fine breadcrumbs. Place in a shallow bowl. Sieve 3–4 tablespoons of flour into another bowl and whisk the egg in a third bowl.

3. Dip each escalope in the flour, shaking off any excess, then in the egg and finally in the breadcrumbs.

4. Heat together the butter and cooking oil over a medium flame 5 minutes before you're ready to eat. When hot, slip in the escalopes.

Cook without moving them for about 2 minutes, flip over and cook the other side – both sides should be crusted and golden.

If not, cook on for a minute or so more. Serve with lemon wedges for squeezing over the top.

Fillets of Plaice with Lemon, Parsley and Peas

Serves 2   *Preparation: 10 minutes. Cooking: 10 minutes*

2 thick slices wholemeal
    bread, crusts removed
flour
1 large egg
4 plaice fillets, approx. 100g
    each, skinned
450g petit pois or courgettes
40g butter

splash vegetable oil
2–3 tbsp freshly chopped
    flat-leaf parsley or mixture
    parsley and basil
2 lemons cut into wedges
salt and freshly milled black
    pepper

Plaice suits simple treatment and swift cooking – just long enough for the flesh to firm up and keep its succulent moistness – so that its distinctive yet subtle flavour can be appreciated. You'd be dead lucky, for example, unless the fillets were spankingly fresh and from a big fish, to get battered and deep-fried plaice that hasn't got a woolly texture from overcooking.

I came up with this quick and simple way of serving plaice fillets after happening upon a van parked up near Wimbledon library recently, selling fish from the south coast – Hastings, I think it was. The two plaice virtually leapt into my bag, and cost about half the price I'd just paid for fillets from my fishmonger's.

Rick Stein's words about the joys of filleting fresh fish were ringing in my ears as I slipped the fish off the bone with unexpected accomplishment. My fillets were vast and one fish easily fed two, but this dish looks better and is easier to cook if the fillets are cut into pieces about the size of a couple of fish fingers.

The fish is dusted with flour, dipped into beaten egg and pressed into fresh, wholemeal breadcrumbs, then fried in butter. It only needs a couple of minutes a side over a medium flame and is delicious when generously covered with plenty of freshly chopped parsley or a mixture of parsley and basil.

If you're feeling River Café-ish, then add a splash of olive oil. The first time I made this, we ate it with peas, the next with lightly cooked blocks of courgette. New potatoes or a decent crust of bread make a mega-meal of it. And don't forget the lemon.

1. Blitz the bread in the food processor to make breadcrumbs. Tip into a shallow bowl or plate. Put about 3–4 tablespoons of flour in another bowl and mix with a generous seasoning of salt and pepper. Whisk the egg in a third bowl.

2. Cut the fillets in half and dip each piece first in flour, shaking off the excess, then into the beaten egg, and finally press into the breadcrumbs to coat evenly on both sides. Lay out the fish as you finish on a plate.

3. Put a large pan of water on to boil. Add salt and the peas. Establish simmer and cook for 2 minutes. Drain, return to the hot pan, cover and leave while you cook the fish.

4. Heat half the butter and a small splash of oil in a frying pan over a medium heat.

When it's bubbling nicely, fill the pan with half the fish. Cook briskly, but without letting the breadcrumbs burn, for about a minute until the fish begins to firm and the breadcrumbs underneath are turning golden.

Turn and repeat on the other side. Transfer to a warm plate and repeat with the remaining fish.

Strew the pieces of fish with the chopped herbs, edge with the peas and serve with the wedges of lemon.

You will need salt, preferably sea-salt flakes, and black pepper.

Lamb's Liver with Parsley, Garlic and Red Wine Vinegar with Potato Leek Gratin

Serves 2   *Preparation: 20 minutes. Cooking: 45 minutes*

For the potato gratin:
450g potatoes
1 large leek
2 tbsp chopped parsley
approx. 275ml water or stock
knob of butter
nutmeg, salt and freshly
    milled black pepper

For the liver:
1 tbsp cooking oil
knob of butter
4 (or more) thin slices
    well-trimmed lamb's liver
2 small garlic cloves
1 heaped tbsp chopped
    parsley
4 tbsp red wine vinegar

This is one of the simplest and nicest ways to eat lamb's liver. It's important though, if the dish is to work as intended, to use very thin slices of liver – ½cm is about right.

The idea is to give it a crusted surface without letting the liver toughen or remain raw, and for this it needs to be cooked quickly in a hot frying pan.

Finely chopped garlic and parsley are added, and the pan is then cleaned out, as it were, with red wine vinegar. This garlicky liquor is poured over the liver and provides an agreeable last-minute sharpness: it's not exactly gravy, more a moist seasoning.

With this you need something fairly bland (creamy mashed potato would be divine), and this potato gratin, made by layering slices of potato and leek with more parsley, plenty of salt and pepper and freshly grated nutmeg, goes very well.

This gratin would make a good supper dish if it were cooked in milk or cream (in which case add a cheese topping or a lattice of bacon); but it is also excellent made with water, or stock if you happen to have some. It's the gratin that accounts for the long cooking time here; the liver is done in a flash and mustn't be kept hanging around. Consequently, this way of cooking liver isn't really suitable for more than two; unless, that is, you eat in relays or you have two pans on the go.

1. Pre-heat the oven to 350F/180C/gas mark 4.

2. Peel, slice and drain the potatoes (don't rinse; the starch makes the slices cling). Trim the leek, slice, rinse and drain.

3. Butter an earthenware gratin dish and make alternate layers of potato and leek, starting and ending with potato, sprinkling each layer with parsley and seasoning. Pour over the stock or water to moisten, not drown, season again and dot with any remaining butter.

4. Bake for 45 minutes or until the potatoes are quite tender and most of the liquid absorbed.

5. Peel and finely chop the garlic. Measure out the vinegar. Pat the liver dry on kitchen paper. Heat half the butter and oil in a frying pan over a medium-high flame and when sizzling nicely, fry two of the slices of liver for 15 seconds, pressing down with an egg slice. Flip over and repeat, and remove to a warm plate.

6. Add the remaining butter and oil to the pan and repeat. Add the garlic, tossing it to turn uniformly golden, stir in the parsley then the vinegar (watch out, it will splutter and its fumes can blast in your face), stir to scrape up any crusty bits, allow to bubble for a moment or two (it evaporates quickly) and pour over the liver. Eat immediately.

Lemon and Almond Turkey with Garlic Runner Beans

Serves 2   *Preparation: 25 minutes. Cooking: 35 minutes*

1 turkey fillet
1 lemon
1 large onion
2 garlic cloves
glass dry white wine
1 scant tbsp Dijon mustard
1 tsp Kikkoman soy sauce
1 tbsp runny honey

3 tbsp blanched almonds
2 tbsp cooking oil
salt and freshly milled black
    pepper
500g runner beans
2 garlic cloves
2 tbsp olive oil

Lately, in an attempt to ring the changes, I've been seeing if I can breathe flavour and interest into minced turkey and the unappetizing slab of pinky-white breast fillet that always seems to be on special offer in the chill counter. And this recipe is a stir-fry made with one fillet which provides ample protein for two people.

I cut the meat across the grain in thin slivers and cooked it with lightly caramelized onion, garlic, lemon juice and white wine.

To add textural variety, I included some lightly toasted whole blanched almonds, and for extra background flavour I seasoned the dish with a little mustard, soy sauce and honey.

Freshness and a different sort of crunch are provided by a big mound of finely sliced runner beans, finished, Chinese-style, in oil and garlic. This would go very well with some plain boiled rice, although rice noodles, too, would be good.

1. Divide the turkey in half lengthways, then slice each half thinly on the diagonal across the grain. Place in a bowl. Use a zester or potato peeler to shave the peel of half the lemon and slice it into thin shreds. Squeeze the lemon juice over the turkey, sprinkle over the zest and use your hands to smear it all over the meat.

2. Peel, halve and finely slice the onion. Peel and finely slice two garlic cloves. Mix the mustard, soy sauce and honey into the white wine.

3. Heat a little of the cooking oil in a wok or large frying pan and when it's hot stir-fry the whole almonds quickly until golden in places. Drain on kitchen paper and wipe out the pan. Return the wok or frying pan to a medium-hot flame, heat the pan and add the rest of the oil. Fling the onions into the pan and stir-fry for 10 minutes until dark brown in places, raising the heat if necessary. Add the garlic and cook for a couple more minutes before adding the turkey. Toss the meat around until it has all changed colour. Add the white-wine mixture, stirring to let everything mix nicely. Turn down the heat and cook at a moderate simmer, stirring every now and again, for 15 minutes. Taste and adjust the seasoning. Add the almonds.

4. Put a large pan of water on to boil. Add 1 teaspoon of salt. Meanwhile, top and tail and finely slice the runner beans. Peel the garlic and finely chop. Fling the beans in the boiling water and cook for 2 minutes. Drain. Heat the olive oil and cook the garlic gently. Turn up the heat and toss the beans with the garlic, taking care not to let the garlic burn – it quickly turns bitter.

Marsala Pork with Sage and Garlic

Serves 2   *Preparation: 15 minutes. Cooking: 30 minutes*

425g pork chump steak	scant ½ tsp salt
3 plump garlic cloves	1 wine glass of Marsala
2 medium onions	salt and freshly milled black
2 tbsp cooking oil	pepper
6 sage leaves	

The most luxurious sage plant I've ever seen grew under the shade of a plum tree and next to the steps that led up to the house where I stayed recently in the Dordogne.

It didn't have the pronounced roughness that is often the case with sage, and the texture of those huge dusty green leaves was marginally more delicate than is usual. When you brushed against this plant or crushed a leaf between your fingers, the smell of its pungent mustiness was almost too powerful to bear.

It's a toughie at the best of times, is sage. Not a herb to sprinkle over a salad – not, that is, unless you've fried the leaves first in oil – and not something to add at the end of cooking.

And you don't need much sage to flavour a dish – it's the same for fresh, dried or dried-out, like the bunch I brought back from France – so it is better to err on the side of caution when seasoning with it.

Consequently, sage goes very well with bland carbohydrates: excellent with dried beans and mashed potato, and perfect mixed with breadcrumbs for stuffings.

Sage loves pork, and in this recipe I've pounded it with garlic and oil to make a paste to marinate chunks of lean meat. Later, these are added to some lightly caramelized onion, and liquid is provided by a glass of Marsala.

This dark sherry-like wine (invented, incidentally, by two brothers from Liverpool in 1773) works well here but could, at a pinch, be replaced by sherry or white wine with a dash of balsamic vinegar. You end up with a sticky sort of dish – add a little water if it seems too dry – which is delicious eaten with smooth and fluffy mashed potato.

1. Trim the pork and cut into decent-sized chunks. Finely chop the sage leaves, discarding the tough central stalk. Pulverize the garlic with the salt and add the chopped sage to make a paste. Mix the paste into 1 tablespoon of the oil.

Using your hands, rub the garlicky sage oil all over the pork.

2. Peel the onions, halve and thinly slice. Heat the remaining oil in a decent-sized heavy-based pan over a medium heat and stir in the onions. Leave them to cook, stirring every now and again, for 10 – 15 minutes until the onions have softened and are beginning to brown in places.

3. Push the onions aside in the dish and add the meat with its marinade. Toss it around until all the meat has changed colour from pink to white and is getting crusted in places.

4. Stir in the Marsala, scraping up any pieces of onion or pork that are stuck, reduce the heat, partially cover the pan and leave to simmer very gently for about 15 minutes, by which time the meat should seem tender when spiked with a small, sharp knife.

Remove the lid, turn up the heat and reduce the juices slightly. Taste and adjust the seasoning with salt and pepper. Serve with mashed potato.

Mediterranean Chicken with Penne

Serves 2−3   *Preparation: 15 minutes. Cooking: 40 minutes*

50g Italian sun-dried red
    peppers
75g Italian sun-dried tomatoes
150ml warm water
1 Spanish onion (approx.
    225g)
16 garlic cloves
225g skinned, raw chicken

2 tbsp olive oil
2 tbsp balsamic vinegar
glass of red wine (approx.
    150ml)
300g penne, tagliatelle or
    another flat pasta
salt and freshly milled black
    pepper

On the one hand, I quite agree with the chef who said to me recently that he couldn't wait for winter, to 'see the back of tomatoes and red peppers', but on the other I never tire of those Mediterranean flavours and I shall be keeping a stash of the rather superior sun-dried tomatoes and red peppers recently available from Merchant Gourmet.

I went the whole hog with Mediterranean flavours for this supper, adding two whole heads of garlic to the contents of a 50g pack of dried red peppers and most of a 100g pack of tomatoes.

The garlic cloves were cooked whole with onions in a little olive oil and then balsamic vinegar, and the dried veg were added with some of their soaking water and a glass of red wine.

With all this I cooked some chunks of chicken and as it simmered away the smells that permeated the kitchen were truly mouth-watering. The quantity of garlic in this intensely flavoured stew sounds alarming, but by cooking them this way they end up tender, buttery and sweet, yet holding their form.

All their harshness is softened into a rich and mellow flavour which won't linger on your breath or give you indigestion.

This is definitely something I shall want to cook when Jack Frost is out and about and a blast of Mediterranean flavours is needed to remind me of summers past and future. This dish goes very well with penne, but tagliatelle or any of the flat, wide pastas would be good.

1. Place the leathery dried red peppers and tomatoes in a bowl and cover with the warm water.

2. Peel and halve the onion and cut into thick wedges. Lay the garlic cloves out on a chopping board and press down on them with the flat of a heavy knife until you hear a crack: the skins will now flake away easily.

3. Cut the chicken into kebab-sized pieces.

4. Heat the olive oil in a Le Creuset-type casserole dish and stir-fry the onions over a medium heat until lightly browned and starting to wilt – 5–6 minutes. Add the garlic and stir-fry for a couple of minutes, then add the chicken. Continue stir-frying until the meat has changed from pink to white, then add the balsamic vinegar.

Let it bubble away while you fish out the dried peppers from the bowl. Slice them in thick bands and when the balsamic vinegar is syrupy add the peppers, tomatoes, soaking water and wine to the pan. Establish a gentle simmer, cover the pan and leave to cook for 20 minutes.

Remove the lid and cook for a further 10 minutes to reduce the liquid slightly. Taste and adjust the seasoning with black pepper – the dried tomatoes and peppers are salty, so take care.

5. Meanwhile, cook the pasta according to packet instructions. When cooked spoon on the sauce and eat.

Mustard Chicken with Sage and Butter Bean Purée

Serves 2   *Preparation: 20 minutes. Cooking: 40 minutes*

1 large onion
4 garlic cloves
1 tbsp olive oil
1 bay leaf
4 rashers smoked streaky
    bacon
4 fresh sage leaves
4 plump chicken thighs
2 tbsp flour
1 glass dry white wine
150ml chicken stock or water

2 tsp Dijon mustard
salt and freshly milled black
    pepper

For the butter-bean purée:
2 cans (approx. 400g) butter
    beans
3 tbsp olive oil
juice of a half a lemon
salt and freshly milled black
    pepper

Every time I go to the supermarket on a shopping-for-basics trip, I find myself loading the trolley with a tray or two of chicken pieces. These get rebagged in sets of two or four and are bunged in the freezer with no particular recipes in mind, but they're always gone by the end of the week.

This recipe was inspired by a rabbit dish cooked by a friend for a large lunch party. My approximation, adapted for chicken, ended up as something quite different, but I think it's more than worth passing on. I added sage where he used rosemary and my freezer stash provided chicken thighs rather than the rabbit legs he'd chosen. My version, I'm sure, was far quicker to cook than the long, slow stew he needed to tenderize those big meaty rabbit legs. It seemed sensible to inject extra flavour so I added a dollop of Dijon mustard and a bay leaf.

The result was a successful combination of tender, juicy pieces of chicken in a golden gravy, laced with mustard, pale strands of silky onion and chunks of salty bacon. I cheated again by using canned butter beans to make the purée (his dried beans were soaked overnight) and that was pretty good, too.

Serve it with equal quantities of spinach and rocket or watercress quickly tossed until wilted in hot, garlicky butter or olive oil.

1. Peel, halve and finely slice the onion. Peel the garlic cloves but leave whole. Roll the sage leaves together and finely shred. Chop the bacon into lardons. Skin the chicken thighs and trim away any fat. Dust all over with flour.

2. Heat half the olive oil in a large pan (big enough to hold the finished dish) and add the onion. Season with salt and pepper and cook over a medium heat until they begin to flop but not colour. After 10 minutes add the garlic, sage, bay leaf and bacon. Cook until the bacon begins to crisp and release its fat. Push all this to the side of the pan or remove if there isn't room, add the remaining olive oil and brown the chicken all over. Pour on the wine and stir vigorously as it bubbles up, then add the stock or water and mustard; return the onion mixture now, if you removed it. Bring to the boil, establish a gentle simmer and half-cover the pan. Cook for 25 minutes, giving everything a good stir a couple of times.

3. To make the butter-bean purée, tip the beans into a colander and rinse with running water. Heat through with 4 tablespoons of water and 1 tablespoon of olive oil. Using a potato masher or mouli-légumes, mash the beans, stir in the remaining olive oil and season with salt, pepper and lemon juice.

Roast Quail with Sage Potato Sandwiches and Quick French Peas

Serves 2   *Preparation: 15 minutes. Cooking: 20 minutes*

4 fresh quail

8 slices prosciutto

2 garlic cloves

4 sprigs fresh thyme

half a lemon

4 tbsp olive oil

2 large potatoes

small bunch of fresh sage

For the French peas:

knob of butter

2 rashers streaky bacon

1 medium onion

1 small garlic clove

2 tbsp water, white wine or
    chicken stock

225g petits pois

3 lettuce leaves

salt, pepper and sugar

Supermarkets have taken to packaging quails in sets of four but they don't risk telling us how many that is supposed to feed. It's a bit mean to offer up one quail to anyone with a decent appetite. I reckon two birds is about right.

I keep a four-pack or two in my freezer for a mid-week treat when I want something quick and easy but a bit special. They go well with polenta – either sitting on a soft, creamy mound of it or on a crusty slab – but it makes sense to do a potato dish that will cook in the oven at the same time. Game chips made with wafer-thin slices of potato work well and so do potato sandwiches. This sounds a daft idea, but slices of potato cut so thin you can see the filling end up crisp round the edge with contrastingly tender centres.

Also from the freezer for our posh quick mid-week dinner comes a pack of peas. To these I've added interest with onion, bacon, garlic and a few shredded outer lettuce leaves, to make a convenience version of petits pois à la française.

1. Turn the oven to 425F/220C/gas mark 7.

2. Peel and halve the garlic and put half a clove into each quail cavity with a sprig of thyme and a squeeze of lemon. Place a sage leaf across the breast of each bird and wrap the entire thing in prosciutto. Place them on a lightly oiled baking tray and brush with a little olive oil.

3. Grease a large baking sheet with a smear of olive oil and tip the rest into a mixing bowl. Peel the potatoes and cut lengthways into thin slices – a mandoline or grater will make short work of this. Rinse the potatoes and drain thoroughly. Put the potato slices into the bowl and, using your hands, smear them thoroughly with the oil. Lay out half the potatoes on the baking sheet, season with salt and pepper and top each one with a sage leaf. Make sandwiches with the rest of the potatoes, tucking small pieces between the two outside layers.

4. Cook the quail on the top shelf of the oven for 10 minutes, then move to a lower shelf and put the potatoes on the top shelf. Cook for a further 10 minutes.

5. Prepare the peas by first dicing the bacon, then peeling and finely chopping the onion and garlic. Melt the butter in a saucepan and stir-fry the bacon, onion and garlic over a medium heat for about 5 minutes until the bacon is cooked and the onion is slightly coloured. Add the peas, 2 tablespoons of water, white wine or chicken stock, and a generous seasoning of salt, pepper and sugar, then cover the pan. Finely shred the lettuce. When the peas are tender stir in the lettuce. When it wilts the peas are ready.

Sardines with Rocket and Tomato

Serves 2   *Preparation: 20 minutes. Cooking: 10 minutes*

4 fresh sardines, gutted but
   with heads on
2 tbsp olive oil
4 ripe, fully flavoured
   tomatoes

4 anchovy fillets
1 tbsp capers, drained
7–10 tbsp olive oil
salt and freshly milled black
   pepper

For the sauce:
90g rocket
a few mint leaves
2 garlic cloves
1 scant tbsp Dijon mustard

For the salad:
90g rocket
1 medium shallot
2 tbsp vinaigrette

Simon Hopkinson, the pioneering head chef of Bibendum, once told me he thought Ian Bates was one of the best natural cooks he knew. Ian is one of the highly talented gang of Simon's ex-sous chefs who've gone on to make their own mark.

This recipe is a variation on a dish that I've eaten several times at the Chiswick in W4 when Ian Bates was chef there – he's at the Bluebird Club now. Basically, it involves grilled sardines, which are laid over sliced tomatoes which in turn are spread with a fresh herb sauce. The fish are almost hidden under a mound of lightly dressed green leaves.

On one visit, coriander dominated the flavours and the garnish was black olives, capers, red onion and diced tomato. Another time it was the flavour of mint that I remember most.

My version is made with rocket, and it was particularly good thanks to the noticeably superior rocket I can buy at my local Cypriot greengrocer, the ever-enterprising Adamou and Sons, just across the road from the Chiswick. If you can't lay your hands on these narrow and very frilly leaves – sold complete with roots – it might be worth adding a handful of watercress leaves in order to replicate their peppery tang.

1. Begin by making the green sauce – you are certain to have too much but it's not worth making any less and leftovers are delicious stirred into pasta. Peel the garlic. Put the rocket leaves, mint, garlic, mustard, anchovies and capers into the bowl of the food processor with a couple of tablespoons of olive oil.

Blitz, scraping down what's thrown up against the side of the bowl and with the machine running, add the rest of the 7–10 tablespoons of oil in a thin stream. You're aiming for the consistency of coarse, green mayonnaise. Season with salt and pepper.

2. Slice the tomatoes, divide between two plates and spoon over 2 tablespoons of sauce.

3. Peel and finely dice the shallot. Toss in the vinaigrette with the rocket.

4. Rinse the sardines inside and out and pat dry with a kitchen towel. Smear the sardines with the 2 tablespoons of olive oil and season thoroughly with salt and pepper. Pre-heat a hob top grill pan (or barbecue, making sure the racks are really hot, or use an overhead grill or a thick frying pan) and cook the sardines quickly with a fierce heat. This takes a couple of minutes a side.

5. Lay the sardines over the sliced tomatoes and top with a mound of rocket and shallot salad. Serve with crusty bread.

Sesame Broccoli Stir-Fry with Chilli, Garlic and Rice Noodles

Serves 2   *Preparation: 15 minutes. Cooking: 10 minutes*

75g rice stir-fry noodles (it looks like white wire wool)

2 medium red onions

2 plump garlic cloves

2 bird's eye red chillies

4 anchovy fillets

400g broccoli

3 tbsp sesame oil or vegetable oil

black pepper

1 heaped tbsp toasted sesame seeds, soy sauce and toasted sesame oil

'There's a wonderful smell of food,' was the parting shot from the Dogfather, my Italian dog walker and an ex-chef, whose post-breakfast visit found me cooking this dish.

It goes without saying that when it comes to stir-fries, it's vital to get all the preparations done before you start cooking. In this case, the first thing you do is put the kettle on.

This is to pour boiling water over some glossy white rice noodles which, I'm pleased to say, can now be found almost everywhere (made, amongst others, by Sharwoods) and not just at the oriental store. They will be ready for draining after just 5 minutes and are an excellent source of instant bulk.

The stir-fry begins with a couple of sliced red onions, wafer-thin slices of garlic, the sliced stalk of the broccoli and, after a couple of minutes, the broccoli florets, which have been cut into bite-sized pieces. Then follows a dedicated few minutes of stir-frying before adding a few chopped anchovies and two finely diced red chillies. Finally, it's time for the drained noodles and a last stir with a sprinkling of toasted sesame seeds.

The dish looks pretty, the silky strands of red onion flopping against the bright green of the quickly cooked broccoli and a shock of broken white 'angel hair', the whole thing flecked with specks of red chilli and golden sesame seeds. It's the sort of bowlful that you can't stop eating and, although it should feed two, it might not. Serve it with soy sauce and, if possible, a few shakes of toasted sesame oil.

1. Place the noodles in a bowl and cover with boiling water.
2. Keeping everything in separate piles, use a small, sharp knife to gouge out the root-and-shoot end of the onions. Halve through their middles and slice through their length to make chunky wedges.

Peel the garlic, halve lengthways and remove the central green germ. Slice the garlic wafer-thin. Split the chillies, hold under running water and wash away the seeds. Chop finely. Chop the anchovy fillets. Now wash your hands in soapy water to remove all evidence of chilli.

3. Remove all the florets from the broccoli stalk and where necessary divide into bite-sized pieces. Trim the stalk and slice into 1cm rounds, then halve the rounds.

4. Heat the wok over a high flame, add the oil, swirling it round the pan. Add the onion, tossing for a couple of minutes until it flops slightly then add the garlic and broccoli stalk, and season with pepper. Keep the food moving, adding the florets 30 seconds later with the anchovy and chilli. Reduce the heat slightly.

After 5–6 minutes of continuous tossing, drain the noodles in a sieve and add them to the pan with a couple of tablespoons of water if the noodles are catching on the bottom. Stir-fry for 30 more seconds, sprinkle over the sesame seeds and tip into a bowl.

Season with soy sauce and toasted sesame oil if available.

Smoked Haddock Hash with Poached Eggs

Serves 2   *Preparation: 15 minutes. Cooking: 30 minutes*

450g belle de fontenay, charlotte or other waxy potatoes
100g rindless streaky bacon
1 bunch spring onions
450g smoked haddock, cut from the middle, skin removed

fistful of flat-leaf parsley leaves
1 tbsp cooking oil
25g butter
2 free range eggs
2 tbsp vinegar
salt and freshly milled black pepper

Smoked haddock, with its dense flesh and powerful flavour, is ideal for hash. I discovered this by default when I (reluctantly) shared the lovely thick fillet of smoked haddock I'd bought for a lone supper (poached with a couple of soft-poached eggs; buttered doorsteps on the side to mop up the milky, buttery juices).

Also lurking in my fridge was a big bowl of boiled French potatoes, a bunch of spring onions, the remains of a bunch of flat-leaf parsley (it keeps better in a sealed plastic bag), a few rashers of bacon and some eggs.

I set to in exactly the same way that I would have done had I been making a corned-beef hash and the results were so successful that I want to pass on the recipe.

I started by frying the bacon – cut into small scraps – and then added diced potatoes, and finally, when the potatoes were beginning to turn crusty, I added the spring onions and fish. After a few minutes, when the chunks of fish had lost their translucence and turned white, the dish was finished.

It is served with a scattering of chopped parsley and topped with a soft-poached egg which, as with the supper I had intended to make, provides a rich and simple 'sauce'. My quantities provide a substantial main course portion for two; so be warned, you probably won't have the appetite for anything else.

1. Place the potatoes in a pan and cook in salted water until tender to the point of a knife.

2. Meanwhile, slice the bacon into lardons. Trim the spring onions and slice the white and tender-green. Run your index finger over the haddock to locate the bones and use tweezers to yank them out. Following the lines of the fillet, slice the fish in strips and then into bite-sized chunks. Roughly chop the parsley.

3. When the potatoes are ready, drain them under cold running water and remove their skins. Dice the potatoes.

4. Heat the oil and half the butter in a large, preferably non-stick frying pan and cook the bacon briskly until crisp. Remove the bacon. Add the potatoes to the pan and cook, tossing them around a couple of times, until they begin to brown and crisp. Stir in the onions with the remaining butter and, as soon as they begin to wilt, add the chunks of fish.

Stir-fry for a few minutes until all the fish has lost its translucence. Return the bacon, season generously with black pepper, sprinkle over the parsley and toss again. Keep warm.

5. Meanwhile, bring a small pan of water to the boil, add the vinegar and establish a simmer. Crack an egg into a cup and slip it into the simmering water, adding the second one in the same way. Cook at a gentle roll for 2–2½ minutes (depending on the size of the egg) until evenly coagulated. Remove with a slotted spoon, and drain over absorbent kitchen paper. Serve a mound of hash with an egg on top.

Tomato and Pesto Tart

Serves 2   *Preparation: 15 minutes. Cooking: 30 minutes*

14 ripe medium-size tomatoes

3 tbsp olive oil

375g ready-rolled puff pastry

For the pesto:

3 tbsp pine kernels

leaves from a large bunch/
   plant basil (at least 60g,
   preferably 90g)

2 garlic cloves

7 tbsp best olive oil

3 tbsp freshly grated
   Parmesan

salt and freshly milled black
   pepper

This excellent tart is vaguely inspired by the perfectly round and crisp tomato and basil galette served at Le Caprice. Their pastry base is thin and elegant, topped with neat slices of peeled tomato scattered with a few basil leaves. Mine is a chunkier relative that's perfect for supper. It too has a buttery, flaky pastry base but mine never seems to end up round and it's spread with a thick layer of home-made pesto before the tomatoes are added. In my version the tomatoes are roasted until slightly collapsed but still juicy, with their flavour concentrated and sweetened.

The joy of this method is that both pastry and tomatoes can be cooked at the same time but only meet just before the tart is eaten, and anyway, the layer of pesto acts as a sort of nappy to the tomato juices. It is also as good cold as it is hot.

You could use any ripe tomato for these tarts – even the dull, immaculately regular red billiard balls that aren't 'grown for flavour' will be magically transformed – but medium-sized, vine-ripened varieties will give best results. There will be left-over pesto but there are plenty of uses for that and it will keep – covered – in the fridge for several days.

1. Turn the oven to 400F/200C/gas mark 6.

2. Immerse the tomatoes in boiling water for 20 seconds. Remove their skins and halve through their middles. Lay out on a lightly oiled sheet of foil on a baking tray. Paint the cut surfaces with a little oil, season with salt and pepper. Place on a bottom shelf in the oven.

3. Cut two 15cm circles from the pastry using a small plate to guide you. Paint one side liberally with olive oil and flip it over on to a foil-lined baking sheet. Prick the unoiled surface all over with the tines of a fork, then oil this surface as before. When the oven is up to temperature, place on a top shelf and cook for 10–15 minutes until the surface is brown and semi-risen.

4. Use an egg slice to flip the pastry disc so the still flabby underside is uppermost. Press down to flatten and return to the oven for a further 5 minutes or until flaky and golden. Flatten the now thoroughly cooked pastry again if necessary.

5. Meanwhile make the pesto. Heat a small, heavy frying pan and stir-fry the pine kernels for a couple of minutes until lightly golden. Peel the garlic. Set aside about ten small basil leaves and place the rest in the bowl of a food processor with the pine kernels and garlic. Blitz. When evenly chopped, with the motor still running, gradually add the olive oil and continue until nicely amalgamated, thick but slack. Transfer to a bowl and stir in the Parmesan to thicken.

6. Using 2 tablespoons of pesto per tart, spread each pastry circle thickly. Cover with tomato halves, nudging them up closely. Strew with the reserved basil leaves and eat.

Yakitori with Cucumber Relish

Serves 2   *Preparation: 20 minutes. Cooking: 30 minutes*

100ml Kikkoman soy sauce
100ml sweet sherry (or dry
   sherry plus 1 tbsp sugar)
1 scant tbsp wine vinegar
3 tbsp sugar
squeeze of lemon juice

1 large cucumber
½ tbsp salt
3 tbsp wine vinegar
1 tsp caster sugar
3 leeks
500g lean chicken

Chicken yakitori is often made with leeks or spring onions inter-spersed between the chicken and it's a revelation to discover just how well either of those goes with the sauce.

All that is required is to cut raw chicken into bite-sized chunks and thread it on to wooden skewers. While the chicken cooks – over a cast-iron griddle, but a heavy frying pan works almost as well – it is basted with a sauce made by reducing soy sauce with sugar and vinegar.

My adapted version using wine vinegar and sherry with the soy sauce results in a good impersonation of the real thing. The flavour is intensely sweet, salty and savoury, with a hint of acidity.

As the perfect foil for these flavours I've chosen a favourite cucumber salad-cum-relish, eaten in quantity as a vegetable.

1. Begin by making the yakitori sauce. Place the soy sauce, sherry, 1 scant tbsp wine vinegar, lemon juice and 3 tbsp sugar in a small saucepan and cook over a medium heat. Stir as the liquid comes to the boil, making sure the sugar dissolves completely. Establish a brisk but gentle simmer and leave to cook away to reduce by just over half and thus thicken and become glue-like, with the consistency of sticky ketchup. This takes about 15 minutes: it will finish thickening as it cools.

2. Using a potato peeler, peel the cucumber and use a mandoline or a sharp knife to cut wafer-thin slices. Spread the cucumber out in a colander, sprinkle with the salt and leave to drain.

3. Bring a large pan of water to the boil. While that's happening, trim the leeks and cut the white and pale-green tender parts into 2½cm lengths. When the water is boiling, add salt and fling in the leeks. Cook at a vigorous boil for 4 minutes or until tender when stuck with the point of a sharp knife. Drain.

4. Next prepare the chicken by removing any skin, fat and sinew, and cut into small kebab-sized chunks. Thread 6–8 pieces of chicken, interspersed with the occasional length of leek (laid horizontally), on to short wooden skewers.

Place the skewers over a prepared barbecue, or in a pre-heated cast-iron ridged hob pan, and cook for 3 minutes a side until the chicken has turned white. Remove the kebabs and use a pastry brush to smear them with the now cooled and very sticky sauce. Return to the grill/pan and continue cooking and lightly basting, turning frequently, for about 6 more minutes, bearing in mind that you want about half the sauce remaining.

5. Finish off the cucumber relish by wrapping the cucumber in a clean tea towel and squeezing out the liquid. Pour the 3 tablespoons of vinegar into a bowl, dissolve the 1 teaspoon of caster sugar and mix in the cucumber.

6. Place the little kebabs on serving plates, pour over the remaining sauce and serve with the cucumber relish on the side.

Suppers for Four and More

Food for sharing with friends; informal, mid-week suppers which are either quick and easy to prepare or can be made with little trouble and left to look after themselves. Many have constituent parts, such as the brown rice pilaf served with cumin lamb chops and minted yoghurt, and the sorrel pesto with poached chicken, wholewheat fusilli and tomato salad, which could form the basis of a vegetarian meal.

After Work Coq au Vin

Serves 4   *Preparation: 15 minutes. Cooking: 65 minutes*

150g streaky bacon
1 Spanish onion
18 pickling onions
2 plump garlic cloves
4 black field mushrooms
8 plump chicken thighs
2 tbsp flour
1 large knob butter and 1 tbsp oil

600ml light red wine such as Beaujolais or Brouilly
1 tbsp redcurrant jelly
3 sprigs thyme
1 bay leaf
salt and freshly milled black pepper
1 tbsp chopped parsley

This is a quick, simplified version of the Burgundian dish that has become a bistro classic throughout the world. It's one of those dishes suitable at any time of year, although we tend to think of it as a winter-warmer. I love it made (and drunk) with a light, dry red wine, when it can be served with new potatoes and runner beans, and those essential peas – a must with coq au vin.

One forgotten and unfashionable tradition is to serve the coq with triangles of bread fried until crisp in butter.

1. Chop the bacon into lardons. Peel, halve and finely slice the onion. Place the pickling onions in a pan, cover with boiling water and leave for 2 minutes. Drain and use a small sharp knife to whip off their skins. This blanching business makes the onion skin easier to remove and stops crying. Peel and chop one garlic clove. Thickly slice the mushrooms. Trim away any flabs of fat and overhanging pieces of skin from the chicken.

2. Heat half the oil in a frying pan and stir-fry the bacon until it begins to turn crusty and the fat runs. Add the sliced onion and cook for 10 minutes until the onion begins to flop. Season with salt and pepper, add the garlic and mushrooms and cook for 5 minutes, turning the mushrooms as they begin to soften. Remove the contents of the pan to a plate. Add the whole onions to the pan with half the butter. Turn the heat quite low, cover the pan, and leave the onions to caramelize slightly, giving the pan a good shake every now and again.

3. While that's happening, heat the remaining oil and butter in a casserole-type dish. Dredge the chicken with flour and fry briskly until the skin is crisp all over; this will take 10–15 minutes. Remove the chicken to the onion plate and pour the wine into the casserole dish with the redcurrant jelly and thyme. Bring to the boil, then return the chicken to the pan. Stir as you bring it back to the boil so that the cooked flour encrusted on the chicken will thicken the sauce. Reduce the heat to a gentle simmer, add all the other ingredients and simmer, uncovered, for 35 minutes. Taste, adjust the seasoning and if you think the sauce isn't thick enough, blend 1 tablespoon of flour into 1 tablespoon of butter and stir scraps of it into the sauce, cooking on for 5 minutes.

Peel and finely chop the remaining clove of garlic and chop again with the parsley. Sprinkle over the coq au vin and serve.

Aromatic Chicken Curry

Serves 4   *Preparation: 30 minutes. Cooking: 40 minutes*

5cm piece fresh ginger
750g tray of chicken
    drumsticks
juice of half a lemon
large knob of butter
2 medium onions
2 garlic cloves
1 level tsp green cardamom
    pods
1 heaped tsp whole coriander
    seeds

1 level tsp black peppercorns
1 level tsp whole cloves
50g creamed coconut
4 tbsp plain Greek-style
    yoghurt
½ tsp ground turmeric
half a chicken stock cube
    dissolved in 150g hot water
salt

If you want to learn about the finer details of making an Indian curry, you'll find no better friend than Camillia Panjabi's *50 Great Curries of India* (Kyle Cathie, £12.99).

Obviously the proportion and balance of spices are what give a curry its distinctive flavour, but the stage at which you choose to add them to the pot is equally important. There are a variety of ingredients that can be used to thicken, colour and flavour the base sauce. Ingredients like coconut, onions, tomatoes and nuts and seeds can create layers of flavour. For example, a highly seasoned curry cooked with red-hot chilli can be softened and sweetened by adding coconut cream towards the end of cooking.

Coconut, in its various processed forms, has all sorts of uses in curries. I've used it creamed in this mild and aromatic version to make a gorgeous thick gravy.

Creamed coconut is a curious ingredient. It looks a bit like a block of frozen lard, but it's a useful thing to have in the storecupboard. You can grate it directly into stir-fries and stewed dishes or dissolve it in warm water to make a substitute for coconut cream or coconut milk.

Unlike canned coconut cream, it won't split when boiled, and once opened keeps for ages. The bad news is that it's more fattening than butter, so use it in small quantities.

1. Use a small, sharp knife to peel the ginger, then grate it. You should end up with a scant tablespoonful.
2. Strip away the skin from the drumsticks and remove all the meat. Cut the meat into bite-sized chunks. Mix the ginger, chicken and lemon together in a bowl.
3. Peel and slice the onions. Peel and chop the garlic. Heat the butter in a pan and gently cook the onions and garlic for about 10 minutes.
4. Meanwhile slit the cardamom pods and remove the seeds. Grind to a powder (an electric coffee grinder is ideal for this) with the coriander, peppercorns and cloves. Sprinkle over the onions and cook for a couple more minutes. Grate the creamed coconut into the onions.
5. Add the meat and mix in all the other ingredients except the yoghurt. Cover and cook very gently for 20 minutes, remove the lid and simmer for 15 minutes until the chicken is tender. Stir in the yoghurt and heat through. Taste and adjust seasonings. Serve with basmati rice, mango chutney and poppadams.

Chicken Confit Renversée with Onion Marmalade and Garlic Mash

Serves 4   *Preparation: 20 minutes. Cooking: 40 minutes*

2 Spanish onions
2 tbsp olive oil
3 tbsp dark brown sugar
2 tbsp redcurrant jelly
1 glass red wine vinegar
1 glass red wine
3 heaped tbsp seedless raisins
    or sultanas
8 chicken thighs

2 tbsp olive oil
900g floury potatoes, such as
    King Edward
3 plump garlic cloves
large knob of butter
approx. 150ml hot milk
salt, freshly milled black
    pepper, nutmeg

Unlike real confit, when all the fat from the chicken, duck or goose, is saved to embalm the meat, in this recipe the chicken is cooked in a hot oven until all the fat runs free. This has a wonderful effect on the meat, making it juicy and tender. And the skin, which is generally the fattiest part of chicken, turns into a crisp salty sheet which is a delectable contrast of textures.

The marmalade is something I make all the time. You'll also find that it can be adapted to whatever you have to hand. By that I mean you could make it with butter or another oil instead of olive oil, or add different fruit for sweetness, and use the dregs of any wine or wine vinegar to give the sour balance.

Onion marmalade is eaten cold and is used like a relish with, for example, pâté or terrine, or with cold meat. I love it spooned into hot mashed potato or pasta with a poached or soft-boiled egg and a sprinkling of fresh herbs. It's also very good on toast as a snack, either on its own or under poached eggs or grated cheese, and is the perfect starting point for building bruschetta or crostini.

1. Turn the oven to 400F/200C/gas mark 6.

2. Trim the chicken pieces, removing any flaps of fat or skin. Assemble the pieces, skin side up, on a cake rack placed over an oven tray. Paint each piece with olive oil and sprinkle generously with salt. Place in the oven immediately without waiting for it to come up to temperature. Cook for at least 30 minutes until the skin is quite crisp and allow it to rest for 5 minutes before serving.

3. For the marmalade, peel, halve and finely slice the onions. Heat 2 tablespoons of olive oil in a wok or large frying pan. When the oil begins to tremble add the onions and stir-fry for 10 minutes until some edges begin to brown. Sprinkle on the sugar and stir until it dissolves. Season generously with salt and pepper then add the wine vinegar, wine and raisins or sultanas. Boil hard then turn down the heat and leave to simmer for 30 minutes. The consistency you're aiming for is thick and jammy, with almost all the liquid gone.

4. Meanwhile, peel the potatoes and cut into even-sized chunks. Rinse, then place in the pan, cover with water. Add 1 teaspoon of salt, establish a vigorous simmer and cook for 10 minutes. Crush the garlic with the flat of a knife, flake away the skin and add the cloves to the pan. Cook for another 10 minutes or until the potato and garlic is tender. Drain, mash and beat in the milk and butter, adding more of either, if necessary, to get the right consistency. Season with nutmeg.

To serve, divide the mash, spoon over a good dollop of onion marmalade and top with two pieces of chicken.

Lemon Mushroom Chicken

Serves 4   *Preparation: 15 minutes. Cooking: 35 minutes*

4 large chicken breasts
juice of 1 large lemon
4 large shallots
25g butter
200g small horse mushrooms

150ml chicken stock (or cube)
150ml double cream
freshly grated nutmeg
salt and freshly milled black
   pepper

For ease of preparation I've made this dish with ready-trimmed chicken breast, but any part of the bird would do.

The chicken is sliced, then briefly marinated in lemon juice while you sauté some diced shallots.

It is a dish that will be delicious made with any mushrooms: you could, for example, make it with a mixed selection of wild mushrooms or 'upgrade' the status of the dish by using chanterelle or some such expensive mushroom.

However, I'm keen on horse mushrooms at the moment – as much to do with their shape as their flavour – but last time I wrote about them my description solicited a mild ticking-off from the Mushroom Bureau (a sort of PR organization for cultivated mushrooms).

So, it is as well to point out that the horse mushrooms you see on sale at Sainsbury's and other supermarkets 'are not grown anywhere near horse-grazed pastures. They are grown inside, on pasteurized straw compost with a peat casing layer on top.'

Anyway, small horse mushrooms (which look like soft, little white rockets and can be found in horse-grazed pastures) are excellent for this dish. They are added once the chicken has had a chance to change colour and before the stock, seasoning and cream.

The sauce cooks long enough for all the flavours to merge, concentrate and thicken slightly, and it provides a luscious creamy lemon background for tender strips of chicken and soft, juicy whole mushrooms.

The perfect accompaniment is fluffy, buttery mashed potato and a green vegetable such as broccoli, French beans or, best of all, perhaps, frozen peas.

1. Slice the chicken across the width in 1cm-wide diagonal strips. Place in a bowl, pour over the lemon juice and toss the chicken around a bit to get evenly coated. Leave to marinate while you attend to everything else.

2. Trim and peel the shallots, dividing the sections as seems natural. Dice finely. Rinse the mushrooms under cold running water, flicking away any peat.

3. Melt the butter in a medium saucepan (preferably a Le Creuset-style heavy-bottomed one) over a medium-low heat, and when it's starting to fizz stir in the shallots. Stir-fry for a few minutes until almost tender but uncoloured.

4. Add the pieces of chicken and lemon juice and cook until the meat is white all over. Add the mushrooms and toss briefly. Season with salt and pepper, pour on the stock and bring to the boil. Reduce the heat immediately and simmer for 10 minutes.

5. Add the cream. Bring back to the boil, reduce the heat again and simmer for a further 10–15 minutes until the sauce seems thick and unctuous. Taste and adjust the seasoning, giving the dish a generous pinch of freshly grated nutmeg too.

Serve when you are ready; this dish will reheat beautifully and can be made pretty with a sprinkling of chives or parsley, but it isn't really necessary.

Creamed Chicken Tagliatelle with Sweetcorn and Thyme

Serves 6   *Preparation: 25 minutes. Cooking: 35 minutes*

8 big chicken thighs

2 plump garlic cloves

small bunch thyme

1 bay leaf

4 black peppercorns

600ml water

2 large onions (approx. 600g)

40g butter

juice of half a lemon

3 large corn on the cob

4 tbsp crème fraîche

1 tbsp finely chopped parsley

700g tagliatelle

salt and freshly milled pepper

In September my greengrocer virtually gives his sweetcorn away and the cobs are big, swollen and firm. He sells them with their fibrous green jackets intact and you have to push aside their silky brown underwear to look at the kernels. These should be plump and tightly packed – always in miraculously neat rows.

Sweetcorn needs to be dropped into boiling water and cooked for 5–8 minutes. Don't be tempted to add salt (or sugar) to the water because this may toughen the kernels.

It's better to season them with sea-salt flakes (not crystals) and plenty of freshly milled black pepper after you dip them into a pat of butter.

For this recipe I cut the kernels off three fine cobs, cooked them with buttery onions and strips of chicken in a lemon and thyme flavoured broth and finished the dish with crème fraîche and parsley.

The mixture of sweetness from the corn, lemon tang to the chicken and hint of thyme in the buttery, creamy juices is very good – so good, in fact, I cooked the dish again the following night.

1. Remove the skin from the chicken thighs and cut the meat off the bone in two or three big pieces. Crack the garlic with your fist and flake off the skins. Pull the leaves off the thyme stalks.

Place the bones, garlic, thyme stalks, bay leaf and peppercorns in a pan with the 600ml water. Bring to the boil and leave to simmer while you prepare everything else.

2. Peel, halve and thinly slice the onions. Soften 25g of the butter in a heavy-based pan over a medium-low flame and stir in the onions with the thyme leaves and a seasoning of black pepper. Cover the pan and leave to sweat, stirring a couple of times, for 10 minutes.

Meanwhile, slice the chicken into 1cm-thick strips. Peel the corn on the cob, rub away the brown silk and trim the root end – a large cook's knife is needed here. Stand the cob on its cut end, hold the pointy end with one hand and use a small knife to cut off the kernels, working round the cob cutting from top to bottom.

3. Transfer the onions to a plate, add the remaining butter to the pan and stir in the chicken. When the meat has turned white, add the lemon juice and sweetcorn.

Stir well for a minute or two as the lemon juice reduces almost to nothing. Return the onions and pour over what should now be about 300ml of chicken stock.

Establish a gentle simmer, partially cover the pan and cook for 15 minutes. Remove the lid and cook for a further 10 minutes to reduce the liquid. Stir in the crème fraîche, taste, add salt and cook for a couple more minutes. Keep warm.

4. Meanwhile, cook the tagliatelle according to packet instructions. Serve with a garnish of parsley.

Poached Chicken with Cracked Potatoes and Guacamole

Serves 4   *Preparation: 25 minutes. Cooking: 1 hour 30 minutes*

1kg ready-washed baby new
   potatoes
1 medium chicken (approx.
   1½kg)
2 carrots
1 medium onion
1 bay leaf
4 cloves
2 branches of thyme or
   rosemary
½ tsp salt
6 black peppercorns
oil for deep frying

For the guacamole:
2 large or 4 small soft
   avocados
3 medium tomatoes, plum are
   best for this
1 small red onion or 4 spring
   onions
2 small green chilli peppers or
   Tabasco to taste
1 tbsp chopped fresh
   coriander
juice of 1 lime
sea-salt flakes and freshly
   milled black pepper

Poaching a chicken is an excellent idea. You end up with tender, moist meat and a couple of pints of stock to use another time. It's also a healthy way of cooking and leaves you guilt-free to serve it with something really fattening.

I got the idea for these potatoes in Sydney at a modest little café-restaurant called Beaches at Balmoral. Little did I realize when I ordered New York fries, as they call them, that I was about to start a new addiction.

1. Cook the potatoes in salted water until tender. Drain.

2. Trim and roughly chop the carrots. Halve the onion through its middle and skewer the bay leaf into one half with the four cloves.

Put them in a pan with the chicken and any giblets, the thyme or rosemary, salt and peppercorns. Cover the chicken with water. Bring to the boil, establish a gentle simmer, cover and leave to cook for 45 minutes.

Turn off the heat and leave to rest for 15 minutes.

3. Allow the potatoes to cool slightly before using your thumbnails to split them in half. It's important not to use a knife for this because you want to achieve an uneven, slightly shaggy edge to the potato halves.

Get the oil really hot, deep-fry the potatoes in batches (overcrowding will stop them browning evenly) and cook until really crusty.

Drain on absorbent kitchen paper, tip into a serving bowl, crumble over some sea salt and keep warm in the oven.

4. To make the guacamole, blanch the tomatoes in boiling water for 20 seconds, cut them lengthways into quarters, slip off their skins, pull out their seeds and chop.

Finely chop the onion and chilli peppers if using.

Cut the avocados in half lengthways, winkle out the stone and use a fork roughly to mash the flesh into its shell. Scoop out with a spoon and transfer to a bowl, mashing further if you think it's necessary. Mix in the other ingredients, cover with clingfilm and store in the fridge until you're ready to serve.

To serve: remove the chicken from the pan, watching out for liquid in its cavity. Remove its floppy skin and divide it up however you like into four portions.

Serve the potatoes and guacamole separately.

Poached Chicken with Sorrel Pesto, Wholewheat Fusilli and Tomato Salad

Serves 4   *Preparation: 20 minutes. Cooking: 25 minutes*

1 medium onion
1 carrot
1 stick of celery
small bunch of thyme
1 bay leaf
6 black peppercorns
pinch salt
300g wholewheat fusilli
1 tbsp olive oil
4 skinless, boneless chicken
    breast fillets

For the pesto:
90g sorrel or young spinach
    leaves

3 tbsp pine kernels
2 plump garlic cloves
7 tbsp best possible olive oil
3 tbsp freshly grated
    Parmesan

For the salad:
2 beef tomatoes
2 tbsp olive oil
1 tbsp balsamic vinegar
1 tbsp chopped flat-leaf
    parsley
salt and freshly milled black
    pepper

It's not until you make your own pesto that you realize what all the fuss is about. Home-made pesto is vibrant green, has a luscious, sensual texture and is so packed with flavour that you'll never buy ready-made again. And when you make it with basil, which is the traditional ingredient, the smell is so powerful it's intoxicating.

Pesto is also incredibly quick to make. And, apart from the fresh greenery, uses convenience ingredients – pine nuts, Parmesan and olive oil – which you're likely to have in the store cupboard.

Sorrel, or tender young spinach leaves, produce a fresh, tangy and subtly flavoured pesto. I used skinless and boneless chicken breast fillets, which I poached in a quickly made aromatic broth acidulated with lemon. The lemon adds flavour but also helps keep the chicken pearly-white, and makes the finished dish stunning to look at.

1. Put a large pan of water on to boil.

2. Peel, halve and slice the onion. Peel and chop the carrot. Roughly chop the celery. Place in a (second) pan with the thyme, bay leaf and peppercorns and cover with 1.2 litres cold water. Season with salt and bring to the boil. Simmer for 15 minutes.

3. When the first pan of water boils, season with salt, add 1 tablespoon of olive oil and the fusilli. Cook at a vigorous boil for 10 minutes, cover the pan and turn off the heat.

4. Heat a small, heavy frying pan and stir-fry the pine kernels for a couple of minutes until lightly toasted. Peel the garlic. Wash the sorrel or spinach and dry. Place the pine kernels, garlic and green leaves in a food processor and blitz. When evenly chopped, with the motor still running, gradually add the 7 tablespoons of best possible olive oil and continue until nicely amalgamated. Transfer to a bowl and stir in the Parmesan.

5. Add the chicken pieces to the simmering broth and cook for 7 minutes. Turn off the heat, cover the pan, and leave while you drain the fusilli and make the tomato salad. Halve the tomatoes, cut into thick slices and arrange on a serving plate. Dribble with the olive oil and balsamic vinegar. Season with salt and pepper.

6. Remove the chicken from the pan (keep the stock to use in another recipe) and cut into thick slices.

To serve, divide the fusilli between the plates, lay over the chicken slices and spoon over a share of the pesto. Sprinkle with parsley and serve the tomato salad separately.

Thai Green Chicken Curry

Serves 6   *Preparation: 15 minutes. Cooking: 30 minutes*

1 tbsp cooking oil	250g green ball aubergines
2 tbsp green curry paste	200g pea aubergines
can of coconut milk	225g sliced bamboo shoots
225ml light chicken stock or	2 tbsp nuoc nam (Thai fish
water	sauce)
6 fresh kaffir-lime leaves	handful of Thai basil leaves
900g lean chicken	a few coriander leaves
6 pink Thai shallots	

For this recipe you will need to visit a Thai food shop or take your chances in Chinatown, where Thai ingredients are particularly well stocked on Saturdays. The largest oriental grocery is Wing Yip (395 Edgware Road, NW2, and 550 Purley Way, Croydon, open until 7 p.m. Mon–Sat and 11.30 a.m.–5.30 p.m. Sun) and others dotted around London are listed in the *Good Food Shop Guide* by Jane Charteris (Evening Standard Books, £9.99).

One vital ingredient which you may have difficulty finding is fresh kaffir-lime leaves. Few people, and that includes owners of several Thai restaurants and shops, seem aware (thank goodness) of a 1993 EC Plant Health Directive which bans the import (but not the sale) of all citrus leaves from non-EC countries. The fact that the leaves haven't been treated with pesticides means they carry a risk of spreading the dreaded citrus pest which, says MAFF, could wipe out a citrus grove in a trice.

They are, however, still widely available but are becoming expensive. If you see them, snap them up (they freeze brilliantly), because their distinctive, haunting limy flavour is severely reduced when the leaves are processed and freeze-dried (now on sale at supermarkets). Wing Yip gets fresh deliveries every Friday, and many oriental shops sell kaffir-lime leaves frozen. Either way, fresh or frozen, give the leaves a wipe before use.

There are as many recipes for Thai green chicken curry as there are cooks to make it. My version includes a generous amount of pea and ball aubergines because I particularly like them. Both are green but have different flavours and textures – the pea is slightly bitter and quite chewy while the ball (also known as African eggplant) is mild, juicy and tender. You could, if you prefer, replace them with green beans or more bamboo shoots, which I like to add for their crunchy texture.

1. Get everything ready and assembled before you start cooking: rinse then roll the kaffir-lime leaves like a cigar and finely shred. Slice the chicken across the grain in bite-sized pieces. Peel, halve and thinly slice the shallots. Pick the pea aubergines off the stalk and rinse. Trim the stalk end of the ball aubergines and quarter. Open the cans of coconut milk and bamboo shoots.
2. Heat a wok or similar and add the cooking oil, curry paste and coconut milk. Stir until it boils then add the chicken stock or water and kaffir-lime leaves. Simmer for 5 minutes then stir in the chicken. Cook at a vigorous simmer for 5 minutes until all the meat has changed colour. Add the shallots and aubergines and continue cooking at a vigorous simmer, giving the pan a couple of good stirs, for 15 minutes until everything is tender. Add the drained and rinsed bamboo shoots and nuoc nam and cook for a couple more minutes. Sprinkle on the basil leaves and coriander. Serve with Thai fragrant rice (350g should be plenty, allowing around 15 minutes' cooking time).

Barbary Duck with Peas and Courgettes

Serves 4   *Preparation: 15 minutes.*
                  Cooking: 30 minutes, plus 10 minutes resting

2 Barbary duck breast fillets
2 tbsp runny honey
1 tbsp soy sauce
6 juniper berries

750g fresh peas
4 medium courgettes
salt and freshly milled black
  pepper

Trying to find out about Barbary duck hasn't been easy. Apparently it's common in France, where it's reared, and according to Frances Bissell, in her useful *Sainsbury's Book of Food*, it's slaughtered at a later stage than most other duck. This gives the meat a more mature and distinctively gamy flavour.

Consequently, Barbary duck requires longer cooking than most other commercially reared duck. Also, because it's a far less fatty meat than the more common Aylesbury, Lincolnshire or Norfolk ducklings, and doesn't come with the usual insulation of a layer of thick fat beneath its thin skin, it can cook up dry if you're not careful.

I bought two Barbary duck breasts from Sainsbury's recently and subjected them to a brief marinade before a good roasting in a hot oven, taking care to baste them more frequently than I'd normally bother.

I went for a sweet–sour combination, mixing soy sauce with runny honey, flavoured with the haunting tang of pine resin, which comes from crushed juniper berries. I let the meat rest for 10 minutes before I sliced it quite thickly and served it with the delicious juices that escaped as I carved.

We ate it with some simply cooked fresh peas and al dente lengths of courgette, and some crusty fried potatoes pressed together into a potato cake. Boiled new potatoes would also go well with the duck, but there's something about the mixture of textures which makes a crisp, fried potato cake worth the effort.

1. Place the juniper berries in a mortar or bowl and use pestle or the back of a spoon to crush and break them up. Mix the honey and soy sauce into the berries and season with a little black pepper.

2. Using a sharp knife, slash the skin of the duck breasts in a cross-hatch without cutting through to the meat. Place the duck on a plate, skin side down, and pour over the marinade, turning the fillets so that the skin gets covered. Leave while you prepare the vegetables and pre-heat the oven to 400F/200C/gas mark 6.

3. Shell the peas. Trim the courgettes and cut each one in half through the circumference. Slice each half into three or four thin lengths.

4. Place the duck fillets, skin side up, on a wire rack resting on an oven tray. Use a pastry brush to paint the skin with the marinade. Roast for 30 minutes, basting the skin at least twice with the remains of the marinade. Remove the duck from the oven, transfer it to a hot plate, cover with a second plate and leave for 10 minutes while you cook the green vegetables.

5. Bring a large pan of water to the boil, add salt and the peas. Boil for 3 minutes before adding the courgettes. Boil for 1 minute, drain and keep warm.

6. Turn the duck so it's skin side down and slice on a slight diagonal across the grain in thickish slices. Divide the meat between four serving plates, dribble over the meat juices and serve immediately with the peas and courgettes and, hopefully, a slice of crisp potato cake.

Cod Chowder with Salsa Verde and Runner Beans

Serves 4   *Preparation: 30 minutes. Cooking: 40 minutes*

6 slices streaky bacon without
   skin
2 tbsp butter
1 Spanish onion
1 large bay leaf
6 large new potatoes (approx.
   750g)
1 tbsp flour
1 glass (150ml) dry white wine
600ml milk
750g thick cod fillet
2 tbsp chopped parsley
750g runner beans
½ tsp salt

For the salsa verde:
50g pine kernels
2 plump garlic cloves
large bunch flat-leaf parsley
10 basil leaves
10 mint leaves
1 tbsp lemon juice
6–10 tbsp olive oil
salt and freshly milled black
   pepper

This chowder has its roots in New England, but I've broken with tradition and thickened it with flour instead of the usual water biscuits.

Generally, with our floury main-crop potatoes, you can rely on their cooking down slightly and helping to thicken the soup, but during the summer months when native potatoes have dense flesh that doesn't disintegrate as it cooks, you need something else to pull everything together. I've also cut down the quantity of liquid and upped the amount of fish, thus turning a soup into a complete meal.

The idea of serving a variation on salsa verde with the chowder was inspired by rouille, which perks up French Mediterranean fish soups. You may prefer to leave it out and stick with the milder flavours, but make sure you have plenty of decent crusty bread to mop and clean the bowl.

1. Slice across the bacon to make thin lardons. Peel and halve the onion, thinly slice one half and finely dice the other. Peel the potatoes and chop into 2½cm chunks. Rinse and drain. Run your index finger down the cod fillet to locate central bones, and remove with pliers or tweezers. Cut the fish into 5 × 2½cm chunks. Thinly slice the beans.

2. Melt the butter in a large non-stick or heavy Le Creuset-type casserole over a moderate heat. Add the bacon and cook for about 5 minutes until the fat runs and the bacon begins to crisp. Add the onion, bay leaf and ½ teaspoon of salt, and allow to soften slightly before adding the potatoes. Sauté without browning for 5 minutes. Sprinkle over the flour, stir until it disappears and mix in the wine. As it bubbles, add the milk, establishing a simmer. Half-cover and cook, stirring every now and again to prevent sticking, testing after 15 minutes, until the potato is tender.

3. Meanwhile, make the salsa verde. Peel and chop the garlic. Place in a food processor with all other ingredients except the olive oil. Blitz to a thick paste then, with the motor running, add the oil in a trickle to make a pesto-like sauce. Taste and adjust seasoning.

4. When the potato is ready, add the chunks of fish, pushing them under the liquid, raise the heat slightly and cook until the fish turns milky white; this will take only 4–5 minutes.

5. Meanwhile, bring a pan of water to the boil, add salt and cook the beans for 2 minutes. Drain.

6. To serve, sprinkle the chowder with parsley. Serve the salsa and beans separately for people to help themselves.

Poached Cod with Sauce Vierge

Serves 6   *Preparation: 30 minutes. Cooking: 55 minutes*

For the court bouillon:
1 tbsp white wine vinegar
1 carrot
1 large onion
1 celery stick
4 peppercorns
1 bay leaf
1 tsp salt
1 litre cold water

For the sauce vierge:
6 very ripe plum tomatoes
2 plump new-season garlic
   cloves
1 tbsp red wine vinegar
salt and freshly milled black
   pepper
200ml good-quality olive oil
a pot of fresh basil
6 thick cod fillets, skin on,
   each weighing about 175g

A few summers ago I spent a week with friends who live in St Tropez. There were many memorable meals, but this sauce, served with warm poached sea bass, was the dish that I couldn't wait to reproduce at home.

It seems a bit misleading to call it a sauce because it's actually more of a salad-cum-dressing or a salsa let down with oil. It's made with olive oil, tomatoes, wafer-thin flakes of garlic and fresh herbs, and its smell, especially if you choose to make it with basil, is quite intoxicating.

When you want to upgrade a simple meal of, say, poached chicken or a plate of spring vegetables, it's the perfect thing to remember.

I often make it specially to serve with hot new potatoes and cold cuts of meat. And for the occasions when you plan to push the boat out with a whole sea bass or cod, sauce vierge is a good alternative to mayonnaise or aïoli.

It has to be made with a good fruity olive oil, preferably extra virgin, and it's also worth seeking out new-season garlic.

Last season's garlic is too pungent for this delicate sauce – but if you do use it, halve it lengthways and pinch out the indigestible green shoot developing inside each clove. It might also be worth blanching the slices in boiling water for a couple of minutes.

The cod is cooked in a court bouillon – a quickly made, acidulated stock. After use it can be strained and used as a fish stock. It freezes well.

1. Peel and finely slice the onion, chop the carrot and celery stick. Place the chopped vegetables in a pan with all the other court-bouillon ingredients and 1 litre of cold water. Bring to the boil and simmer for 20 minutes.

2. Peel and slice the garlic in wafer-thin rounds.

3. Mix together the vinegar, salt, pepper and garlic in a serving bowl.

4. Blanch the tomatoes in boiling water for 20 seconds, cut them lengthways into quarters, discard their skins, core and seeds, and chop the flesh into dice.

5. Stir the chopped tomatoes into the bowl and leave to macerate for 30 minutes.

6. Tear the basil leaves into pieces. Stir in the basil and olive oil.

7. To cook the fish, bring the court bouillon to the boil, slip in the cod fillets and bring back to the boil. Simmer for 10 minutes, turn off the heat and leave for 10 minutes. Take the fish out of the pan and remove the skin. Spoon the sauce over the fish and serve with mashed potato and, perhaps, green beans.

Linguine with Fiery Prawns

Serves 3–4　　　　　　*Preparation: 10 minutes. Cooking: 15 minutes*

400g linguine
½ habanera chilli pepper
bunch of spring onions
2 garlic cloves
1 tbsp chopped coriander
　　leaves
1 tbsp chopped flat-leaf
　　parsley

400g can of tomatoes
6 tbsp olive oil
400g raw giant Tiger prawns
　　in their shells
sea-salt flakes and freshly
　　milled black pepper
1 large lemon, quartered
　　lengthways

As luck would have it, I happened to catch a trailer for *Fruits of the Sea*, Rick Stein's second television series. In it, Rick made a very simple Italian dish with linguine, mussels, olive oil, garlic, chilli and parsley which made me want to cook it immediately.

I didn't, of course, because I forgot all about it – or so I thought until recently, when, faced with preparing a quick pasta supper, I found myself reaching for a packet of frozen prawns and cooking a variation on that mussel dish.

The preparation takes a few minutes – peeling prawns, chopping chilli, garlic, spring onions and herbs – and the actual cooking not much longer once the pasta has cooked.

I used habanera chillies from my branch of Sainsbury's, and although very hot, they have a pleasing fruity flavour. The chilli is fried in the olive oil with garlic, onion and about half the herbs before the prawns are added and cooked briefly until they change colour from grey to pink.

Next, I added a can of chopped tinned tomatoes to the pan and merely heated them through, before stirring this mixture into the hot drained pasta. The dish is seasoned with a little salt and plenty of black pepper and served sprinkled with the remaining herbs and a wedge of lemon to be squeezed over the pasta just before it's eaten. Excellent.

1. Put a big pan of water on to boil. Add salt and the linguine, following packet instructions but reckoning on about 8 minutes cooking time. Drain and return to the cooking pan, tossing with 1 tablespoon of the olive oil. Cover and keep warm.

2. Chop the chilli very finely (wash your hands carefully after this – these chillies can burn). Trim the spring onions and slice all but the toughest green part quite finely. Peel the garlic and slice into thin rounds. Drain the tomatoes and roughly chop, wiping away some of the seeds.

3. If using frozen prawns, slip them into a bowl of warm water for a few minutes and then remove their shells (which, if you're feeling diligent, could be boiled up to make an excellent stock that can be frozen). Almost split the prawns lengthways so they open out butterfly-style.

4. Heat the oil in a large frying pan over a medium-high heat and quickly fry the garlic, onion and half the herbs, before adding the prawns. Cook, stirring all the while, as they change colour from grey to pink, then stir in the chopped tomatoes and heat through.

5. Tip this into the pasta, returning the pan to the heat, toss for a few seconds, stir in the remaining herbs, season with salt and pepper and serve with a wedge of lemon to be squeezed over the pasta just before it's eaten.

Salmon, Leek and Dill Jalousie

Serves 4   *Preparation: 20 minutes. Cooking: 25 minutes*

3 medium leeks
1 tbsp butter
squeeze of lemon, or splash of
   white wine or Noilly Prat
2 tbsp chopped dill
350g ready-made puff pastry

2 × 200g plump salmon fillets,
   skin and bones removed
1 egg yolk, beaten with a
   splash of milk
salt and freshly milled pepper

Picture, if you will, a puffed and golden louvred pastry. It is oblong in shape and large enough to feed four people. Through the slats you can glimpse pale green, and the steam that rises gives off enticing wafts of buttery pastry, mingled with leeks and salmon, with a background hint of aniseed from aromatic dill.

When you cut into this flaky pastry, you will see a thick fillet of salmon sandwiched in a mound of tender, pale-green leeks flecked with dark fronds of fresh dill. The fish will be cooked just-so; firm and beginning to flake at the edges, but still holding its dark pink colour. It won't have that rather too-white finish and fall into crumbly dry flakes in the way that salmon often does. Apart from its sheer deliciousness, this dish has many other points to recommend it.

It most certainly looks impressive, both before and after it has been sliced but, more importantly, it is foolproof to make and quick to cook. There is also something immensely satisfactory about a dish that will be as good cold as it is hot.

In fact, it is almost worth making two and serving one hot with boiled potatoes and peas, and the other cold with a dainty cucumber salad, soured cream and yet more dill. Even more satisfactory is the fact that this splendid dish can be made well in advance and won't suffer from being kept a while in the fridge.

1. Place a flat baking tray in the oven and pre-heat to 425F/ 220C/gas mark 7.

2. Split the leeks twice from root to stem and wash under running water. Shake dry and chop. Melt the butter in a lidded pan, stir in the leeks, cover and leave to sweat gently for 5 minutes.

Stir, adding the lemon juice or wine or Noilly Prat, season with salt and pepper and return the lid. Cook for a few more minutes until tender, then remove the lid to drive off most of the liquid. Tip on to a plate and leave to cool, then mix in the dill.

3. Lightly flour a work surface. Cut the ready-made pastry dough in half and roll one piece to make a rectangle 30½ ×15cm and the other to measure 28 ×12½cm.

Fold the larger half lengthways and cut across the fold at ½cm intervals, leaving a 1½cm border. Transfer the uncut rectangle of dough to a second flat baking tray, sprinkled with cold water.

4. Spoon half the leek filling evenly down the centre, leaving a 1½cm border and lay the fish – trimmed to fit if necessary – on top of the leeks, season with salt and pepper and cover with the remaining leek.

5. Use a pastry brush to moisten the border with water. Line up one long edge of the slashed dough rectangle with one long edge of the pastry on the baking sheet and unfold to make a lid. Press the border edges together.

Brush the whole surface with the egg wash and go round the border again, this time with the tines of a fork, pressing firmly.

6. Place the tray and Jalousie in the oven over the pre-heated tray and bake for 25 minutes until puffed, golden and spectacular.

Serve in crosswise slices.

Lime-Scented Prawn Summer Salad

Serves 4   *Preparation: 20 minutes. Cooking: 10 minutes*

1 medium onion
6 dried kaffir-lime leaves
4 peppercorns, pinch salt
200g raw Tiger prawns
570ml water
200g snow peas or mange tout
half an iceberg lettuce
12 cherry tomatoes
2 heads chicory
1 lustrous bulb fennel

½ cucumber
2 tbsp chopped mint
2 tbsp snipped chives
1 tbsp roughly chopped
    coriander leaves
1 heaped tbsp mayonnaise
4 tbsp vinaigrette
squeeze of lemon
salt and freshly milled black
    pepper

Where would we be without fresh herbs? Fresh herbs are my greatest extravagance. I use them in just about every savoury dish I make, I even keep a stash of quick-frozen herbs (Daregal are available at Safeway, Waitrose and large branches of Sainsbury's) for emergencies.

I buy most of my herbs, certainly dill, flat-leaf parsley, coriander and mint, from a Cypriot greengrocer because they sell proper big bunches, not the mimsy little polythene envelopes and the weak, spindly pot herbs usually on offer at the supermarket.

It makes a welcome change, as one of my local shops has done, when a greengrocer makes herbs a speciality. At Macken & Collins, Turnham Green Terrace, they stock fourteen varieties, all available in proper-size bunches.

The best way to keep most fresh herbs, incidentally, is in separate spacious polythene bags at the bottom of the fridge.

Coriander also needs to have its roots in a jar of water and mint keeps better wrapped in foil.

This salad is a lovely mixture of textures and flavours and goes very well with hot, peeled new potatoes and/or some good brown bread with decent butter.

1. Peel, halve and slice the onion and place in a pan with the peppercorns, a pinch of salt and 570ml water. Crumble in the kaffir-lime leaves, add the prawns and bring the water slowly to the boil (allow 10 minutes for this). As soon as the water boils vigorously, turn off the heat, cover the pan and leave while you prepare everything else.

2. Bring a second pan of water to the boil, add ½ teaspoon salt and throw in the snow peas or mange tout. Boil hard for 1 minute (30 seconds if using mange tout), drain in a colander and hold under cold running water for a couple of minutes. Leave to drain.

3. Halve the cherry tomatoes. Trim the root end of the chicory and slice into 1cm rounds. Halve the fennel lengthways, cut out the tough core and slice finely across the middle. Finely chop any frondy leaves. Finely slice the cooked snow peas or mange tout on the slant in the style of preparing runner beans: you should get about four long slices per pea. Put the mayo into a salad bowl and stir in the vinaigrette to make a thick dressing.

4. Strain the prawns, reserving one tablespoon of the liquor to stir into the salad dressing: if you wish, the remains can be frozen for use in a later prawn dish. Peel off the prawn shells and throw the warm prawns in with the salad dressing. Season with black pepper and a squeeze of lemon, stir, taste and adjust the seasoning if necessary. Mix in all the other ingredients, reserving the chives to sprinkle over the top.

Barbecue Salmon, Tabbouleh and Minted Peas with Cucumber

Serves 6   *Preparation: 30 minutes. Cooking: 9 minutes*

6 salmon fillets, skinned
1 tbsp olive oil

large bunch flat-leaf parsley
small bunch mint

For the tabbouleh:
225g cracked wheat/bulgar
juice 1½ large lemons
½ tsp salt and freshly milled
    black pepper
4 tbsp olive oil
6 drops Tabasco
4 spring onions
2 large ripe tomatoes

For the peas:
400g fresh peas, shelled
    weight
½ cucumber
4 good branches fresh mint
large knob butter
juice ½ lemon
salt and freshly milled black
    pepper

One time-honoured way of preserving the flavour of fresh herbs is to steep them in vinegar or oil. Herb flavours take around three weeks to be absorbed into vinegar and work best with wine or cider vinegars. Simply stuff clean and prime herbs – dill, thyme, basil, bay, garlic, lemon balm, chive, mint or tarragon – into the bottle, recork and leave to steep before straining off into a clean bottle.

Flavoured oils require a bit more attention. Crush the leaves slightly, place in a jar and pour over the oil, giving the jar a good shake every day for a couple of weeks. Then strain into clean, dry bottles. Use to dribble over pasta and pizza, to anoint simply cooked courgettes and other summer veg, and in marinades and vinaigrettes.

1. Use your hands to smear the salmon fillets with olive oil, lay out on a plate and protect from flies.

2. To make the tabbouleh, pour the cracked wheat/bulgar into a colander and wash under cold, running water until the water runs clear. Tip the cracked wheat into a large bowl then pour over enough boiling water to cover by 2½cm. Cover and leave for 30 minutes. Drain in a colander, shaking vigorously and pressing with your hand to get rid of all the water.

3. Pour the lemon juice into a salad bowl, dissolve the salt, add the Tabasco and season well with black pepper. Whisk in the olive oil to make a thick, creamy dressing.

4. Mix the drained cracked wheat into the dressing.

5. Trim and slice the white and soft green part of the spring onions very finely. Pour boiling water over the tomatoes, count to 20, drain, quarter, peel and remove seeds. Dice. Mix onions and tomatoes into the cracked wheat. Taste and adjust the seasoning – it needs masses of salt.

6. Pick all the leaves off the parsley and mint and chop. Mix into the tabbouleh.

7. Next the peas. Peel the cucumber and halve it lengthways. Use a teaspoon to gouge out the seeds and slice into thick half-moons. Roll the mint leaves like a cigar and finely slice. Place all the ingredients, except the lemon and a little of the mint, in a small pan with 2 tablespoons of water. Cover and simmer vigorously for 3 minutes. Taste, adjust the seasoning with lemon juice, stir in the remaining mint and serve.

8. Pre-heat the barbecue racks, lay on the fish and cook for 3 minutes per side until the salmon turns several shades lighter on the outside but is still moist and dark inside.

The Dish (with apologies to Katharine Whitehorn)

Serves 3–4   *Preparation: 15 minutes. Cooking: 45 minutes*

1 lamb fillet
1 lemon
2 medium onions
1 plump garlic clove
2 carrots
1 fennel bulb
10 small new potatoes

1 tbsp cooking oil
1 can tomatoes
1 tbsp chopped marjoram
1 tbsp chopped parsley
200g peas, shelled weight
salt and freshly milled black
    pepper

In the Sixties, the cookery book that everyone in the know just had to have was Katharine Whitehorn's slim little Penguin called *Cooking in a Bedsitter*.

Her pragmatic and amusing style was a breath of fresh air in a world where most cookery books were wrapped up in etiquette and 'principles of good cooking'. She broke the rules, providing realistic recipes which might rely on stock cubes and gravy mixes but were grounded in good taste and a knowledge of Elizabeth David.

'As far as I'm concerned,' she wrote, 'the chefs of the world labour in vain to bring themselves up to the standards of a single cold potato eaten out of the larder in the middle of the night.'

Many of her recipes, which evolved while sharing a house with five other girls, were one-pot dishes that could bubble away while she was doing something more interesting. The most famous of these is simply called The Dish. ('So called because my flat-mate and I cooked almost nothing else for nearly two years. We left it on all night once by mistake, and it still made a lovely ragout.')

My Dish is a similar idea with Greek overtones. I've used lamb, rather than beef, and cooked it over direct heat rather than in the oven. I've tailored my version to cook relatively quickly and used summer vegetables and fresh herbs for flavouring and to pretty it up. You could, however, use any vegetables you like so long as you keep the onion and tomatoes. Red pepper – essential to the original – works well, and so would aubergines in place of the carrots and fennel. A handful of black olives will make it even better.

This is the sort of dish that improves overnight – kept covered in the fridge – and leftovers could be frozen.

1. Peel, halve and then slice the onions. Peel and slice the garlic. Trim and peel the carrots and cut on the slant into chunky slices. Trim the fennel, cutting out the core at the base, and slice. Split the lamb fillet lengthways in two. Chop the lamb into large kebab-sized chunks. Scrape the new potatoes. Use a knife to roughly chop the tomatoes in the can.

2. Use a pan that can hold all the ingredients and place over a medium flame. Heat the cooking oil, and toss the meat around in the pan until it's browned on all sides. Squeeze over the lemon juice and add all the vegetables, tomatoes and marjoram and half the parsley.

Season very generously with salt and pepper, bring to the boil and then turn down the heat so the stew bubbles away gently.

Leave for 30–40 minutes until the juices have reduced into a thick, succulent gravy and all the vegetables are thoroughly cooked.

Taste and adjust the seasoning.

Add the peas 10 minutes before you're ready to eat.

Sprinkle over the reserved parsley and eat with crusty bread.

Lamb Kebabs, Hummus, Pickled Cucumber and Baked Potatoes

Serves 4   *Preparation: 30 minutes. Cooking: 30 minutes*

For the pickled cucumber:

1 large cucumber
½ tbsp salt
4 tbsp red wine vinegar
2 tsp caster sugar

For the hummus:

420g can chickpeas
juice of 1 lemon
2 garlic cloves
1 tbsp tahini (optional)
5 tbsp olive oil

salt
Tabasco
½ tsp ground cumin

For the kebabs:

500g lamb neck fillet
1 garlic clove
½ tsp salt
juice of 1 lemon
2 tbsp olive oil
lemon wedges

When Simon Hopkinson and I were writing a book together we worked at my place. Our plan was an early start, and if the morning went well we'd reward ourselves with a late lunch at a favourite restaurant.

In reality we didn't get out for lunch very often. Hunger pangs would strike mid-morning so lunch had to be something that could be sorting itself out while we worked.

One of our favourite combinations was baked potatoes and hummus with chilli relish.

Simon's way of cooking the potatoes, which I've now adopted, is to place them on an oven tray which goes into a cold oven turned to the highest possible setting. If the potatoes are cut in half and rubbed with olive oil, they are ready for eating in about 30 minutes.

A good tip is to dip the cut side into flakes of Maldon sea salt. This cooks up attractively and gives the potatoes a more-ish savoury crust.

Another good thing to eat with hummus and baked potatoes is pickled cucumber.

Add lamb kebabs and you have one of the best combinations of textures and flavours I know.

1. Slice the cucumber wafer-thin into a colander. Dredge it with salt and leave for 20 minutes. Rinse thoroughly, then use your hands to squeeze out all the water. Mop up the last of the moisture with absorbent kitchen paper. In a bowl or jam jar, dissolve the sugar in the vinegar. Mix in the cucumber.

2. To make the hummus, peel and chop the garlic. Drain and rinse the chickpeas. Blitz both with the lemon juice, garlic, tahini, if using, and a little water, to form a thick paste. Gradually add the olive oil. Season with salt, Tabasco and cumin. Spoon into a bowl.

3. To make the kebabs, trim away any big pieces of fat from the lamb and cut it into 2½cm cubes. Peel then chop the garlic and pound it to a paste with the salt. Put the paste in a mixing bowl with the lemon juice, then, using a wooden spoon, beat in the olive oil. Tip the meat into the bowl and use your hands to smear the cubes with the garlic oil. Then thread the meat on to wooden skewers. Lay the skewers on a hot griddle (ridged hob-top grill pan) or place them under a pre-heated overhead grill. Cook, turning them every few minutes, until the meat is nicely crusty.

Serve the kebabs with lemon wedges, a dollop of hummus and a mound of cucumber.

You'll need chilled butter for the baked potatoes.

Brown Rice Pilaf with Cumin Lamb Chops and Minted Yoghurt

Serves 4   *Preparation: 15 minutes. Cooking: 35 minutes*

2 heaped tbsp flaked almonds
2 tbsp vegetable oil
handful of broken vermicelli
small knob of butter
225g long-grain brown rice
2 heaped tbsp sultanas
600ml vegetable stock or
    salted water
2 Spanish onions

4 garlic cloves
1 tsp cinnamon powder
8 small lamb chops
1 tbsp olive oil
1–2 tbsp cumin
salt and freshly milled black
    pepper
Greek-style natural yoghurt
fresh mint

This is a recipe that I've been cooking for twenty years and I've yet to tire of it. I first came across it in an eccentric hand-written American cookbook called *Naturally Good* by David and Marlena Spieler, published here by Faber and Faber in 1973.

To be honest I haven't really been interested in trying other pilaf recipes because this one seems to me to be spot on.

I tweak it here and there, sometimes adding sliced mushrooms (towards the end of cooking the onions), or raisins instead of sultanas, and almond flakes rather than whole almonds, and as I love onions I double the quantity, but that's it.

By default, I discovered that it's just as good cold, so it's a useful dish to make up in quantity for a party. I often serve it with garlicky stewed aubergine but like it best with lamb that's been rubbed with garlic and olive oil and sprinkled with cumin.

1. Heat ½ tablespoon of the vegetable oil in a small frying pan and sauté the almonds until uniformly golden. Wipe out the pan and repeat with the vermicelli. Drain both separately on absorbent kitchen paper.

2. In a lidded saucepan, stir-fry the rice in the butter and cook until the grains are golden, then add the sultanas, stock or salted water and the pasta. Bring to the boil, cover the pan and simmer over a low heat for about 35 minutes until the rice is al dente.

3. Meanwhile, peel and finely slice the onions and two garlic cloves. Heat the remaining vegetable oil in a large frying pan and gently sauté the onions and garlic over a medium heat until limp and slightly brown in places; allow about 30 minutes. Season with the cinnamon, then fork the mixture into the pilaf along with the almonds.

4. Prepare the chops by crushing the remaining two garlic cloves to a paste with ½ teaspoon of salt and mix it into the olive oil. Use your fingers to smear the garlic oil over both sides of the chops. Lay the chops out in the grill pan, sprinkle with cumin and cook until aromatic and crusty. Turn, sprinkle on more cumin and repeat.

Serve with a dollop of yoghurt laced with finely chopped fresh mint.

Lamb 'Tortilla' with Salad and Spicy Tomato Sauce

Serves 4   *Preparation: 15 minutes. Cooking: 30 minutes*

For the lamb:
1 large onion
1 head celery
1 scant tbsp cooking oil
1 tsp celery seeds (optional)
1 tbsp dried oregano
500g minced lamb
juice of half a lemon
1 tbsp red wine vinegar
salt and fresh black pepper

For the chilli sauce:
400g can tomatoes
1 red chilli pepper
3 garlic cloves

1 tbsp tomato ketchup
slug red wine
salt and pepper
2 firm ripe tomatoes

For the salad:
1 beef tomato
½ iceberg lettuce
2 large ripe avocados
juice of half a lemon
50g mushrooms
2 carrots
100g mature Cheddar
1 tbsp chopped mint leaves
4–8 pitta bread

Tortilla is a bit like thin pizza or chapati, and when made with wheat flour, as opposed to corn, it's immensely versatile, and not just in Mexican cooking for dishes such as fajita, burrito, enchilada and taquitos. They can, for example, be used instead of crêpes or pastry, and work just as well for sweet things as they do for savoury.

The trouble is, although tortilla is easy to make and very economical, it takes about 30 minutes of concentrated effort to conjure up enough for four. There are several passable ready-made versions available at the supermarket, but all contain preservatives or ingredients with alarming quantities of E numbers. Instead, for this recipe I've improvised with pitta bread.

The recipe is related distantly to all manner of Mexican dishes and uses the warmed pitta bread to sandwich celery-flavoured minced lamb and a selection of salady ingredients and grated cheese. It is delicious and very messy to eat.

1. Peel, halve and slice the onion. Use the root half of the celery and chop it finely – slice the rest thinly, on the slant, for the salad. Heat the oil in a pan over a medium heat. Fry the onion for 5 minutes, then add the celery, celery seeds, if using, and oregano. Cook, stirring occasionally, for 10 more minutes then raise the heat and add the lamb. Stir-fry until the meat changes colour, squeeze over the lemon juice and vinegar, and season with salt and pepper. Lower the heat slightly and cook for 15 minutes, adding a little water if it seems dry.

2. Crack the garlics but don't bother to peel them, and place in a pan with all the other sauce ingredients except the two tomatoes. Boil hard, giving it a couple of good stirs while breaking up the tomatoes at the same time. Cook for around 15 minutes until the liquid is reduced by at least half. Remove the chilli then pour and push the mixture through a strainer – boil again if it seems watery. Cover the fresh tomatoes with boiling water, count to twenty, drain, peel and chop, then add to the sauce. Transfer to a jug.

3. And now the salad. Slice the tomato. Shred the lettuce. Peel and core the avocados, slice and smear with lemon juice. Slice the mushrooms. Grate the carrots and Cheddar. Arrange everything, including the celery, in separate piles on a large platter. Sprinkle with chopped mint.

4. Warm the pitta until puffy and floppy. Slit one side. Serve the lamb hot, the sauce lukewarm or cold, and the pitta warm.

Tagliolini with Herb Sausage Meatballs, Roast Tomatoes and Caramelized Onion

Serves 4   *Preparation: 30 minutes. Cooking: 30 minutes*

4 medium tomatoes,
   preferably plum
2 tbsp olive oil
salt and fresh black pepper
2 sprigs thyme
1 large onion
lemon
225g good-quality pork
   sausage meat (possibly best
   taken from sausages)

1 egg yolk
1 tbsp chopped chives
1 tsp chopped sage
1 tsp chopped thyme
250g Cipriani or Spinosi
   tagliolini
3 tbsp Boursin or similar
   cream cheese
fistful of chopped basil leaves

It's always a bit tricky writing recipes involving obscure pasta. I could, of course, simply say pasta, and describe the most suitable shapes and thickness. But that gets a bit boring.

The very finest tagliolini is sold beautifully packaged in boxes under the Cipriani and Spinosi labels, both of which are available in some supermarkets and specialist food shops. Spinosi is available mail order from 0800 137064.

This silky pasta is made with a high proportion of egg and the best quality durum wheat flour, and its superb flavour and texture are worth its high price tag. It cooks just as quickly as fresh pasta and swells magnificently during its brief cooking. These gorgeous golden strands go wonderfully well with what was actually a supper of leftovers and turned out to be a delicious combination.

It might easily be a dish from one of those new-wave restaurants: you know the sort of thing, when the menu reads as if the chef has been playing lucky dip with the cuisines of the world.

The cooked pasta is stirred with fresh basil and moistened with a dollop of Boursin or a similar cream cheese, then topped with a mound of caramelized onions, a couple of roasted tomatoes and a few tiny, herb sausage meatballs.

A few more freshly snipped basil leaves add the final touch.

1. Pre-heat the oven to 400F/200C/gas mark 6.

2. Halve the tomatoes, lay out on foil on a baking sheet, smear with olive oil, season with salt and pepper and lay the thyme sprigs across the tomatoes. Cook in the hot oven for 20 minutes.

3. Peel, halve and finely slice the onion. Fry gently in 1 tablespoon of the olive oil for about 10 minutes, season with salt and pepper and cook for a further 5 minutes until limp with crusty edges. Set aside to cool.

4. Use a potato peeler to remove a length of zest from the lemon, chop finely and add to the bowl with the sausage meat, chives, sage, thyme, egg yolk, salt and pepper. Squeeze over the lemon juice. Use your hands to mix everything together into a clump.

5. With wet hands, pinch into tiny lumps of mixture and form into cherry-sized balls.

Heat a frying pan, add the remaining oil and cook the meatballs until nicely crusted, allowing about 6 minutes for this. Cook the pasta in plenty of salted boiling water (it takes 2–3 minutes), drain, stir in the cream cheese and half the basil.

6. To serve, divide the pasta between four hot plates or bowls, pile up with a share of the onion, tomatoes, meatballs, a dollop of cream cheese and sprinkling of basil.

Pork and Onion Kebabs with Lentil Salad

Serves 4–6   *Preparation: 20 minutes. Cooking: 40 minutes*

For the lentils:

225g Puy lentils

¼ chicken stock cube

1 medium onion

2 cloves

1 bay leaf

600ml water

generous pinch cumin

3 medium tomatoes

squeeze of lemon

2 tbsp best olive oil

salt and fresh black pepper

For the marinade:

2 plum garlic cloves

1 medium onion

small bunch thyme

½ tsp dried oregano or 1 tbsp
    chopped marjoram

4 tbsp olive oil

juice of 1 large lemon

1 bay leaf

2 pork tenderloins

500g small (pickling) onions

It is always difficult to give quantities for food that is going to be cooked over a barbecue because everyone seems to eat so much more than usual.

Normally I'd reckon on one tenderloin (they average 400g) feeding three people when it's combined with other foods, but when I made this recipe, four of us made short work of two tenderloins. And that was when it was accompanied by this hearty lentil salad, a green salad and crusty bread.

Tenderloin lives up to its name and is tender and succulent meat that's almost entirely lean. When sliced thin and cut into medallions or slivers, it cooks in seconds and a little seems to go a long way in a stir-fry. It has a naturally sweet flavour and, like all pork, goes with all sorts of flavours.

When tenderloin is cut into chunks and barbecued it needs a marinade. Not only does the marinade add flavour: it helps to lubricate what can easily turn into dry meat.

It's worth searching out French Puy lentils for this dish because their pronounced flavour and dense texture are far superior to that of other lentils.

The combination of succulent and crusty-edged chunks of aromatic pork with sweet tender onion and the almost earthy taste of the lentils is particularly good.

1. Begin with the lentil salad. Wash the lentils and place in a saucepan with the stock cube and the (peeled) onion stuck with the cloves securing the bay leaf. Cover with 600ml water and season with salt and pepper. Bring to the boil and simmer for about 30 minutes until the lentils are tender and the liquid absorbed. Peel, de-seed and dice the tomato and mix into the lentils with the cumin. Season with salt, pepper and lemon juice.
2. While the lentils are cooking, peel, chop then crush the garlic to a paste with a little salt. Grate the onion. Mix together with all the other marinade ingredients. Remove the band of fat on the underside of the fillet, divide into three strips the length of the fillet and slice into small cubes. Mix the meat into the marinade.
3. Pour boiling water over the onions. Leave for 1 minute, drain, splash with cold water and use a sharp knife to remove the peel. Throw into a pan of boiling water and cook for 5 minutes until the onions are tender. Drain.
4. Thread the meat on to skewers, interspersing with onions. Baste the entire kebab. For best results the barbecue coals should be white before cooking starts. Cook for about 2 minutes a side, basting at least once, until the edges are crusty.

Serve the warm or cold lentils with some of your finest olive oil.

Stuffed Pork Parcels

Serves 4   *Preparation: 30 minutes. Cooking: 15 minutes*

4 loin pork chops, with or
    without bone
juice of 1 small lemon
225g fresh spinach
25g pine kernels
2 tbsp cream cheese

salt and freshly milled black
    pepper
freshly grated nutmeg
2 tbsp cooking oil
1 tbsp butter
flour for dusting

This is a neat way of adding interest to pork chops. What you do is slip a sharp knife into the fatty edge of the chop and slide it about to make a pocket into which you stuff anything you think would go well with pork, though it must be something that needs only to be warmed through.

Scraps of salty bacon or prosciutto are good, on their own or mixed with a few chopped mushrooms or shredded cooked greens, as are some finely diced mushrooms sweated in butter with shallots and tiny shreds of lemon zest. There again, a few very soft prunes swollen with port would be delicious.

My choice is soft, crunchy and creamy – a combination of cooked spinach, pine kernels and cream cheese. The spinach could be fresh or frozen (make sure to squeeze out all the liquid) and the pine kernels will contribute far more interest if they're toasted first. A generous pinch of freshly grated nutmeg, too, will make quite a difference.

I've chosen boneless loin medallions, and they can be cooked in the oven (with frequent basting), fried or grilled on a hob-top grill pan. If you happen to have some breadcrumbs handy, then egg and breadcrumb the chops before frying in plenty of oil and butter, and they end up looking like crisp, golden pillows.

Either way, the chops will be excellent with a couple of (fried or grilled) big black field mushrooms and baked potatoes.

1. Using a small, sharp knife, make a 2½cm horizontal slit in the middle of the fatty edge of each chop. Work the knife sideways and forwards, going right up to the edges, but leaving a ½cm border, thus creating a sealed pocket which is almost the size of the chop.

Lay on a plate, squeeze lemon juice over and inside the chops and set aside.

2. Wash the spinach and chuck into a pan of vigorously boiling salted water. Cook for 30 seconds, drain in a colander, hold under the cold tap for a few seconds and drain again.

3. Gather the spinach up in your hands and wring out the water. Chop it roughly, place in a mixing bowl and season generously with salt, pepper and nutmeg.

4. Heat a heavy frying pan over a medium ring with a smear of the given oil and toss the pine kernels until lightly but evenly biscuit-coloured. Tip on to kitchen paper to drain, then add to the spinach along with the cream cheese. Use your hands to mulch everything together.

5. Remove a chop from its lemon bath, drain and, using a teaspoon, stuff it with a quarter of the spinach mixture. Pinch the edges closed and, if necessary, use a wooden toothpick to secure the opening. Repeat with the other chops.

6. Dust with flour, shaking off any excess. Heat the butter and oil in a frying pan until seething, and cook the chops for 3–5 minutes a side, adjusting the heat so the meat is cooked to your liking. Serve with lemon wedges.

Sausagemeat Patties with Fresh Tomato Sauce and Deep-Fried Onion Rings

Serves 4   *Preparation: 30 minutes. Cooking: 20 minutes*

2 bunches spring onions

2 garlic cloves

large knob butter

8 fresh sage leaves

1 eating apple

500g pork sausagemeat

flour for dusting

1 egg, separated

5 tbsp fresh breadcrumbs

1 tbsp milk

1 tbsp cooking oil

500g ripe tomatoes

2 tbsp tomato ketchup

1 tsp sugar

small bunch chives

1 Spanish onion

oil for deep frying

salt and freshly milled black
    pepper

I unzipped Cumberland sausages to make these tasty little patties, but any decent pork sausagemeat would do. It's seasoned with sage, apples and onions, all ingredients familiar with pork. The mixture is then formed into ping-pong-sized balls and flattened into patties about a third the size of a burger. They fry up well, but if you bother to dip them first in egg yolk and then in breadcrumbs there's the bonus of a delicious crunchy coating.

I love the combination of cooked and uncooked tomato and this quick, half-cooked tomato sauce goes well with the patties.

All you really need with this is some sautéed potatoes or chunky pasta. It was the egg white, left over from making the patties, that gave rise to the onion rings. This is such a simple idea: all you do is dip the onion in whipped egg white and once they hit hot oil they puff and turn golden in seconds.

1. Trim away the roots and coarse dark leaves of the spring onion. Slice finely. Peel and chop the garlic.

2. Melt half the butter in a saucepan that can also hold the tomatoes. Stir-fry the onion and garlic for 5 minutes.

3. Put the sausagemeat in a mixing bowl. Season with salt and pepper and add half the spring onions. Peel, core and grate the apple. Finely chop the sage leaves. Use a fork to work everything together. Cut the mixture into four and form each quarter into three balls. Flatten slightly in the palm of your hand, then lay them out on a plate and dust lightly with flour on both sides.

4. Pour boiling water over the tomatoes, count to twenty, peel and roughly chop. Add to the pan with the reserved spring onions. Add the ketchup, sugar and seasoning and boil hard for 5 minutes. Add the chives.

5. Whisk together the egg yolk and milk in a cereal bowl and put the breadcrumbs in a second bowl. Dip the patties first in the egg and then in the breadcrumbs. Heat the butter and oil together in a frying pan and cook the patties over a medium heat for 2 minutes, then lower the heat and cook for 5 minutes until golden brown and obviously cooked through. Turn and repeat.

6. Whisk the egg white until it is stiff. Heat at least 5cm of the oil in a pan while you peel the onion and slice into ½cm-thick rounds. Separate the rings. Dip each onion ring in egg white, dust with flour and toss into the hot oil. When they turn golden brown remove with a slotted spoon and drain on absorbent paper.

Serve the patties piled with onion rings, with the tomato sauce on the side.

Pork and Sage Meatballs with Apple Purée and Chestnut Gemelli

Serves 4 *Preparation: 30 minutes. Cooking: 30 minutes*

For the meatballs:
1 shallot
1 garlic clove
1 small lemon
10 fresh sage leaves
4 tbsp white breadcrumbs
2 tbsp thick cream
knob of butter
1 egg
1 tbsp finely chopped parsley
450g minced pork

1 chicken stock cube dissolved
    in 400ml water

For the apple sauce:
2 Bramley cooking apples
wine glass of water
25g butter
1 tbsp sugar
300g chestnut gemelli
    (Maestri Artigiani)
salt and fresh black pepper

Gemelli is a short pasta, not as stubby as penne, folded and twisted back on itself like two intertwined lengths of long macaroni. The chestnut variety looks like wholewheat pasta and is something you'll find in Italian grocers. I chose it specially to go with these tiny pork meatballs, which are flavoured with the zest and juice of lemon, garlic, shallot, parsley and quite a lot of sage.

Although essentially a meaty meatball, they are enriched and extended with breadcrumbs mixed with cream, and the mixture is bound firmly with beaten egg. Forming the mixture into balls is a satisfying task and easiest done with wet hands, pinching off pieces and rolling them between the palms into cherry-tomato-sized balls.

Once ready, the little balls could be kept in the fridge for up to twenty-four hours before use (on a covered plate), and there is the choice of poaching or frying them. If you fry, you end up with pleasingly crusted edges and consequently more pronounced flavours.

Also complementing the albeit slight flavour of chestnut, which goes so well with pork, lemon and sage, I went for a tart apple purée to serve as a lubricating sauce as well as adding its fresh, clean flavour to this delicious combination.

1. Peel and dice the shallot. Peel and finely chop the garlic.

Use a potato peeler to remove four strips of lemon zest and finely chop. Roll up the sage leaves like a cigar and finely chop. Mix the breadcrumbs into the cream.

2. Melt the butter in a frying pan and gently soften the shallot, adding the garlic after a couple of minutes, without colouring. Cool, then tip into a mixing bowl containing a beaten egg before adding the lemon zest, juice of the lemon, parsley and sage, breadcrumbs, cream and pork. Season well with salt and pepper.

3. Use your hands to mix everything together into a clump. Divide into four and, working with wet hands, form seven balls from each piece. Lay out on a plate.

4. Peel, quarter, core and quickly chop the apples. Place in a pan with the water, cover and boil hard until collapsed. Stir in the butter and sugar and keep warm.

5. Cook the pasta in boiling salted water according to packet instructions.

6. Meanwhile, bring the stock to the boil in a medium pan, add the remaining lemon juice and drop in the meatballs. Bring back to a simmer and cook for 10 minutes.

7. Drain the pasta, serve in warm bowls with a generous dollop of apple purée and a share of the meatballs.

Pork and Onions in Aromatic Wine with Porcini

Serves 4   *Preparation: 30 minutes. Cooking: 40 minutes*

300ml white wine
small bunch fresh thyme
1 bay leaf
2 garlic cloves
25g dried porcini/ceps
300ml hot water
400g pork escalope
juice of 1 lemon

40g butter
3 large onions, preferably Oso
1 tsp chopped sage
1 heaped tbsp flour
200g double cream
salt and freshly milled black
   pepper

This is a recipe that benefits from left-over wine not quite good enough to drink but more than adequate to turn what might have been an ordinary supper dish into something a bit special.

It is worth cooking up wine with other flavourings before it's added to the dish, and in this case I did so with a small bunch of thyme, a bay leaf and a clove of garlic.

Meanwhile, I marinated strips of pork escalopes in lemon juice, then added them to a mound of butter-softened onions with chopped sage and garlic. At the same time, I rehydrated some dried porcini in hot water and added that when ready to the pork and onions, and thickened the mixture with a little flour.

The porcini-soaking liquid and aromatic wine are strained into the dish and everything left to simmer and thicken before adding some thick cream. The end result is a rich, unctuous sauce flavoured by the aromatic wine with a hint of lemon and sage, all undercut by the pronounced mushroom hit from the porcini-soaking water, not to mention the porcini themselves.

The onion cooks down to a silky slop and, if you've used deluxe Oso onions, they will hardly have coloured at all.

Though my description of this dish sounds like a lot of palaver, in fact each stage is straightforward and the delicious result worth the effort. It's the sort of dish that goes with almost anything and would be good with boiled new potatoes, mash, pasta or pommes frites. Best of all, perhaps, would be buttery wide noodles tossed with chives and dusted with nutmeg

1. Place the wine, thyme, bay leaf and one garlic clove (crushed lightly and peeled) in a small stainless steel or enamelled pan. Simmer gently until reduced by half.

2. Place the porcini in a small bowl and cover with the hot water. Leave to soak for 20 minutes.

3. Slice the pork into 1cm-wide strips, place in a bowl and squeeze over the lemon juice, tossing to coat evenly.

4. Peel, halve and slice the onions.

5. Melt the butter in a heavy bottomed casserole dish over a medium-low flame. Stir in the onions and the sage, and season with salt. Peel and chop the remaining garlic and add to the onions. Cook for about 20 minutes until the onions begin to soften but not colour. Now add the pork.

6. Scoop out the porcini, reserving the liquid, and add to the casserole dish. Sift over the flour, stirring to prevent lumps.

7. Strain over the wine from the pan and the porcini-soaking liquid and bring to the boil while stirring continuously to make a smooth sauce. Establish a simmer and cook for 15 minutes or until the meat is tender.

8. Stir in the cream, taste, and adjust the seasoning with salt and pepper. Cook for another few minutes and serve.

Chickpeas, Tomatoes and Spinach with Spicy Garlic Pork

Serves 4   *Preparation: 15 minutes. Cooking: 30 minutes*

3 large garlic cloves
350–450g pork fillet
1 tbsp olive oil
400g can Italian whole
   tomatoes
425g can chickpeas
350g young leaf spinach
salt and fresh black pepper

1 tsp West Indian Hot Pepper
   Sauce, or 1 tsp dried chilli
   flakes
squeeze of lemon juice
fistful chopped coriander
   leaves

This dish couldn't be easier, quicker to make, or more delicious. It doesn't involve much 'cooking', by which I mean fiddling with ingredients. That's not to say it's what is often described as a 'cheat's' recipe; rather, it utilizes two excellent convenience products – canned Italian tomatoes and chickpeas.

There are just two provisos. One is that it's worth paying extra for Italian tomatoes (I prefer whole canned tomatoes because I reckon you get a better deal), which come as close as possible to the real thing. The other is always tip your can of chickpeas into a sieve or colander and rinse them thoroughly before use.

Now, back to supper. Chunks of pork fillet, which cook very quickly, are smeared with a little olive oil and masses of very finely chopped garlic crushed with salt. It's all then fried fast and furiously to get nice crusty edges, then cooked up with a can of roughly chopped tomatoes, chickpeas and a decent splash of West Indian Hot Pepper sauce or a generous pinch of dried chilli flakes.

After about 20 minutes at a steady simmer, the seasoning is

adjusted with pepper and lemon juice, and what seems like far too much young leaf spinach is squashed into the pan. The moment the spinach has begun to flop – literally seconds later – a handful of fresh coriander leaves is added, and that's it.

This hearty, full-flavoured, stewy sort of meal-in-a-bowl is great with a hunk of crusty bread and butter. Big appetites might also like some boiled new potatoes added to the pot.

1. Peel and chop the garlic, discarding the green central germ. Sprinkle with salt and use the flat of a knife to work to a paste.
2. Slice the meat into kebab-sized pieces and place in a bowl. Use your hands to smear first the oil and then the garlic all over the meat. Then wash your hands.
3. Open the can of tomatoes and slice through the contents a couple of times while still in the can. Open the chickpeas and tip into a colander or sieve and rinse well in cold running water. Rinse the spinach and shake dry.
4. Choose a heavy bottomed pan for this dish – Le Creuset or similar is ideal – and get the pan very hot over a medium flame. Tip in the meat and its marinade and allow to go crusty without stirring (and thus not stick – if it does, don't worry). When all sides are crusted, tip in the tomatoes and chickpeas and season with pepper sauce or chilli flakes, stirring up the meat.
5. Establish a lively simmer and cook for about 20 minutes until the meat is tender and the tomatoes have almost entirely flopped and formed a thick, jam-like sauce still with pieces of tomato.
6. Taste and adjust the seasoning with pepper and lemon juice. Add the spinach, stirring into the sauce, and as soon as it begins to wilt, stir in the coriander and serve.

Puddings

When someone tells me that they think nobody eats puddings except on high days and holidays, I don't believe them. In my house, there's an uproar if there isn't a pudding of some sort, and I'm talking day in and day out (what a weird expression). We might have changed our habits away from suet pud and semolina towards fruit and yoghurt, but sometimes, why shouldn't a luscious fresh pineapple custard, plum clafoutis or tarte tatin *be* supper?

Apple Tart with Crème Fraîche

Serves 4   *Preparation: 20 minutes. Cooking: 10–15 minutes*

250g fresh ready-rolled puff
   pastry
4 Cox's apples
1 lemon
1 tbsp caster sugar

2 tbsp icing sugar
1 tsp cooking oil
knob of butter
crème fraîche to serve

Toad in the hole, bangers and mash, beef stew with dumplings, apple tart and stewed rhubarb with custard. Food you cook at home or dishes from some of London's most fashionable restaurants?

Not so long ago all these dishes were regarded as humble, everyday sort of food and if any of them appeared on menus it was in clubland, gentlemen's clubland.

Generally speaking, restaurant and home interpretations of dishes are always going to differ.

In a fashionable restaurant, like, say, Alfred, where they serve toad in the hole, it's a whole different ball game. Their butcher makes up special high-pork-content Cumberland sausage which is pre-cooked, sliced on the slant, arranged in individual servings and hidden beneath a soufflé-style super-light batter. It arrives with veal-stock braised-onion gravy.

This kind of revivalist cooking is welcome indeed, but who cares to go to so much trouble for a weekday supper dish?

Every now and again there is a restaurant dish that is so quick and easy that it translates to the domestic kitchen with ease.

One such dish, with the extra bonus of being very economical, is what the restaurant Lou Pescadou calls La Tarte aux Pommes Minute.

Almost a play on words, this tart takes 10 minutes or so to cook, and is an individual Normandy-style apple tart on a wafer-thin pastry base. They serve it flambéed at the table with a generous dousing of Calvados.

Le Caprice does a similar tart with a dollop of sweetened whipped cream and calls it Tarte aux Pommes Chantilly.

1. Pre-heat the oven to 475F/240C/gas mark 9.

2. Dust a suitable flat surface with flour and roll out the puff pastry very thinly. Cut out four circles using a saucer as a guide. Sprinkle a little water on an oiled baking sheet and lay out the circles of pastry. Lightly prick the pastry all over with the tines of a fork to stop it rising as it cooks and pushing off the apples.

3. Squeeze the lemon juice and caster sugar into a mixing bowl. Peel, core and slice the apples into thin segments. As you work, place the slices in the sweetened lemon juice to stop them from discolouring. Cover the pastry with the slices in overlapping concentric circles, French-apple-tart-style, to cover entirely the pastry circles. Then dredge each tart with icing sugar and dot with a little butter. Place in the hot oven and cook for 15 minutes, checking for doneness after 10 minutes.

Serve, hot, warm or cold with crème fraîche on the side.

Baked Apricots with Almond Yoghurt Rice

Serves 4   *Preparation: 15 minutes. Cooking: 45 minutes*

800g apricots
1 vanilla pod
3 tbsp caster sugar
2 tbsp water
1 knob butter
225g basmati rice

300ml Neal's Yard Dairy
    Greek yoghurt
3 tbsp toasted flaked or
    shredded almonds
caster sugar

I'm convinced that the best thing to do with apricots that are not yet ready to eat is to cook them in the oven, the slower the better. They will be heavenly if you halve them, pluck out the stone, lay them cut side up in a buttered baking dish, smear them with a little butter and almost fill the cavities with sugar. Let them bake in a low oven (300F/150C/gas mark 2) for 45–60 minutes and they'll taste like apricots ought to and have a little crusty filling.

To make more of this idea, try filling their cavities with crushed amaretti (or full-sized macaroons) and softened butter mixed to a paste with an egg yolk and dusted with sugar.

I wanted this concentrated apricot flavour in stewed form to serve with a creamy rice concoction which is a current addiction. For the rice, all you do is cook basmati until it's dry and the grains are separate. Then stir a goodly dollop of full-fat Greek-style yoghurt into the rice, season it generously with caster sugar and add a garnish of toasted almonds.

Several Iranian food shops have sprung up near where I live in west London. They keep superb stocks of nuts and pickles and very superior chunky shredded almonds which are ideal for this.

This pudding is so simple, so good and much richer than you'd imagine possible – especially if you use Neal's Yard Dairy Greek yoghurt. When the rice is topped with these vanilla-scented apricots, you have a combination made in heaven.

1. Pre-heat the oven to 300F/150C/gas mark 2.

2. Use a small knife to follow the natural line of the apricot and split sufficiently to whip out the kernel but leave the two halves hinged. Butter a baking dish, sprinkle with one tablespoon of caster sugar and pack the dish with the apricots. Break or bend the vanilla pod between the apricots, sprinkle with the rest of the sugar and dribble over two tablespoons of water. Place in the middle of the oven and cook for 30 minutes or until the apricots have shed some juice and are juicy and tender. Remove from the oven and leave to cool while you cook the rice.

3. Wash the rice and place in a pan with double the volume of water. Allow to boil, then immediately turn down the heat and clamp on a lid. Leave undisturbed to steam/simmer for around 15 minutes until all the water is absorbed and the grains are tender and separate.

4. Spoon 4 heaped tablespoons of rice into four serving bowls and stir 3–4 tablespoons of yoghurt into the rice to make a creamy mixture. Season with caster sugar and garnish with almonds. Mix everything together.

Serve the bowl of apricots, a bowl of caster sugar and the rest of the yoghurt for people to help themselves. This is good hot or cold but is best when rice and apricots are tepid: this happens very quickly anyway.

Cherry and Almond Flan

Serves 4–6   *Preparation: 30 minutes. Cooking: 40 minutes*

500g plump, ripe,
   ruby-coloured cherries
100ml water
100g whole almonds
100g caster sugar
2 eggs
almond flakes (optional)

For the pastry:
8 heaped tbsp plain flour
100g butter
2–4 tbsp cold water

The shops are full of the most wonderful cherries most summers: big, juicy and full of flavour. Of the American varieties there are five with distinctly different qualities and colour, including an early variety called Bing. These are huge and plump with a deep-ruby skin and sweet, rich, full flavour.

They make compulsive eating as they are, but when baked in the oven in a pie (500g cherries to 300g puff pastry in a hot oven for 15 minutes) or blanketed by pancake batter to make the French classic clafoutis, they're something else.

This recipe is one that I've known and loved for years and comes from my prized 1970 edition of Margaret Costa's *Four Seasons Cookery Book* (given to me by Simon Hopkinson, who was given his by Delia Smith; sorry about this name-dropping, but it's interesting because of the influence Mrs Costa has had on these two).

This remarkable book is packed with superb, workable, seasonally linked recipes, and I'm delighted it has recently been republished by Grub Street. I can't recommend it enough.

In this flan – such an awful word – the cherries are covered in a gloop made by mixing ground almonds with sugar and egg. Even though I've reduced the quantity of sugar (from 150g) it sets firm, but is spongy and almost cake-like.

While I was fiddling about trying to stone the cherries, I hit upon a foolproof method. Stab the non-stalk end with a potato peeler – the thin, swivel type – twist it round and gouge out the stone.

It works like a dream and took 6 minutes to stone 500g of Bing. To remove cherry stains from fingers, rub with lemon (purple turns red) and wash with soap and water.

1. Pre-heat the oven to 375F/190C/gas mark 5.

2. Make the pastry first. Sift the flour into a bowl, cut the butter into pieces and, using your fingertips, work quickly into the flour. Using a knife (or fork if you're superstitious) stir in the water, a little at a time, until it forms into one big lump. Knead quickly, sprinkling over a little more flour if it seems too loose. Roll out on a floured surface and line an oiled or nonstick 20½cm metal flan case with the pastry. Cover the pastry loosely with foil, fill the dish with rice or dried beans (to stop the pastry from rising) and bake for 10 minutes in the hot oven.

3. Rinse the cherries and remove their stalks and stones (see above). Place in a pan with the water, bring to the boil, cover the pan and turn off the heat. Leave while you grind the almonds and whisk the eggs. Mix the almonds with the sugar and eggs to make a soft paste.

4. Drain the cherries and arrange in the part-cooked flan case. Pour over the almond mixture, spike with almond flakes if liked, and bake for about 30 minutes until the top is a pale-golden colour and set.

Serve cold with a big dollop of crème fraîche or Greek yoghurt.

Fig Frangipane Tart

Serves 6   *Preparation: 30 minutes. Cooking: 30 minutes*

175g plain flour
75g cold butter
approx. 4 tbsp cold water
extra butter or oil

For the frangipane:
75g blanched almonds
2 eggs
35g caster sugar
50g butter
6 ripe figs
1 tbsp extra caster sugar

I was just admiring a bargain-buy of twenty perfectly ripe figs when a friend, who is lucky enough to have a particularly productive fig tree in her garden, rang to pick my brains about what she could do with her annual glut.

It is hard for me to imagine getting bored with figs *au naturel* because I'm too mean to splash out on them that often. I do, though, think that the sheer sensual pleasure of burying your mouth in the soft, smooth skin of a ripe fig, its succulent grainy flesh yielding against the tongue, is one of life's great indulgences.

My figs are lined up, laid out squat and swollen on a white dish, waiting, perhaps, to be eaten with a sheet of Parma ham or a slab of feta cheese. Figs have a natural affinity with creamy foods (excellent with *petit-suisse* sprinkled with caster sugar), port (if you ever see them bottled in port, this is one for the store cupboard), and nuts.

They bake well, snuggled up closely in a buttered shallow dish, slashed and glazed with melted butter and sugar, and basted with a glass of port. They need only 15 minutes in the oven and should be eaten cool with crème fraîche or apricot purée, or both.

This recipe is a way of making the most of six ripe figs. They are sliced and rest on an almond custard in a thin, crisp, shallow shortcrust-pastry case.

Half an hour in the oven sets the frangipane and concentrates the flavour and sweetness of the figs.

1. Pre-heat the oven to 400F/200C/gas mark 6.

2. To make the pastry: sift the flour into a large mixing bowl. Cut the 75g cold butter into small pieces and use your fingers to rub it quickly into the flour until it resembles heavy breadcrumbs. Add the water, a little at a time, until, using a knife or fork, you can stir it up into a clump.

Flour a work surface and roll the pastry until you can cut a circle to fit a 25cm tart tin. Butter or oil the tin thoroughly and tuck the pastry into position, using scraps to plug any tears or cracks. Trim the edges, cover loosely with a sheet of foil and half-fill with rice or dried beans.

Cook for 10 minutes, then reduce the oven temperature to 350F/180C/gas mark 4. Remove the foil and return the tart to the oven for 5 minutes.

3. Make the frangipane by processing the almonds to a dust and mix with the sugar, creamed with eggs and butter. When the pastry case is lukewarm, pour in the frangipane, smoothing it out to cover the base evenly.

Slice the figs in thick rounds – about four to each fig – and arrange to cover entirely the frangipane. Sprinkle the sugar over the top and return to the oven for 30 minutes.

The tart is done when the frangipane is set and what you can see of it is beige.

Allow to cool and dust with icing sugar before serving with crème fraîche or Greek yoghurt.

Figs in Red Wine with Walnut Custard

Serves 6   *Preparation: 10 minutes, plus at least 30 minutes cooling.*
Cooking: 45 minutes

2 ×250g ready-to-eat dried
   figs
1 bottle fruity red wine
4 sprigs fresh thyme
2 tbsp runny honey

3 tbsp caster sugar
50g walnut pieces
1 carton M&S fresh custard
4 tbsp double cream (optional)

Recently, a friend loaned me Jeremiah Tower's *New American Classics*, published by Harper and Row in 1986. Although its design seems dated compared with today's cult chef books with their sharp graphics and in-your-face photographs, the content is bang up to date and offers many 'new' ideas.

This is the kind of chefs' cookbook I find compulsive; not only do the recipes sound interesting and achievable, but they – and the acres of chat that go with them – are packed with tips and informed anecdote.

This recipe, which I've simplified only slightly and relied on Marks & Spencer's excellent ready-made fresh custard, is a good example of Jeremiah Tower's wit in teaming ingredients.

Ordinary dried figs are stewed in red wine, sweetened with honey and sugar, and flavoured further by thyme. These are served with custard mixed with ground walnuts. In both cases, the results are stunning: the figs and their liquor are both sweet without being cloying with a hint of thyme, and the custard is transformed beyond belief.

It reminded me of chocolate praline, when the chocolate has

been mixed with finely grated almonds, giving it a richness that isn't particularly nutty but is altogether luxurious and creamy with a slightly grainy texture.

This recipe is stunningly simple and a real wow; a perfect dinner-party pud that can be made in advance. In fact, it will positively improve if left to sit for several hours.

1. Pre-heat the oven to 300F/150C/gas mark 2.

2. Put the figs in a stainless steel or enamelled saucepan and pour over the wine. Add the thyme, honey and sugar. Place over a low–medium flame and bring slowly up to simmer, stirring with a wooden spoon as the sugar dissolves. Leave to simmer for 30 minutes.

3. Meanwhile, lay the walnut pieces on foil placed on a baking sheet and toast in the hot oven for 10 minutes. Allow to cool slightly and then rub the pieces between your hands to get rid of the flaky husks.

4. Tip the nuts into a food processor and blitz to a fine paste. Tip the custard into a small saucepan and scrape the walnut paste out of the food-processor bowl and into the custard. Warm through, over a low flame, just sufficiently to stir in the paste but without losing the thick texture of the custard. Transfer to a serving jug or bowl.

5. Remove the figs from the pan with a slotted spoon to a serving bowl. Remove the thyme and simmer the cooking liquid until reduced by about one-third and noticeably thicker. Don't, however, let it burn and caramelize. Strain the liquid over the figs and allow to cool.

6. If using the cream, whip it lightly and stir into the custard. Serve the figs lukewarm or cold, with the custard separately.

Fresh Pineapple Custard

Serves 6　　　　　　*Preparation: 20 minutes. Cooking: 40 minutes*

1 knob butter

1 vanilla pod

600ml milk

1 large pineapple (approx.
　1.2kg)

3 large whole eggs

3 large yolks

3 tbsp sugar

2 tbsp flour

2 tbsp crème fraîche or
　double cream

Bistro Cooking by Patricia Wells is one of my favourite books and I could happily live on its recipes, working my way through each chapter and savouring such dishes as L'Amis Louis roast chicken, Brasserie Flo's roast duck with tomatoes, olives and mushrooms, and Tante Paulette's sweet pear omelette.

It was an unexpected glut of bargain pineapples that prompted me to have a go at Flan à la Ananas Adrienne (devised by Adrienne Biasin of Chez La Vieille).

It is really no more than pineapple chunks and custard, but in this version the custard cooks in the oven over the pineapple.

It looks fantastic when it emerges from the oven, the egg slightly puffed, yet wobbly and scorched in patches where the pineapple juts out to make geometric patterns.

Fortunately, it is very simple to make and, although the quantities involved are supposed to feed eight, there were no leftovers when I made it for six.

This would be a lovely finale to Sunday lunch or, dare I say it, a good thing to have up your sleeve for Christmas. According to Patricia Wells, you are supposed to be able to turn this out on a rack to cool. My slightly adapted version seemed far too delicate for that and, anyway, we ate it right away, dusted with a sprinkling of icing sugar.

Extra crème fraîche isn't necessary, but I'd serve it if I were you.

1. Pre-heat the oven to 400F/200C/gas mark 6.

2. Give the vanilla pod a good bash to release its seeds, place it in a saucepan with the milk and bring to the boil. Turn off the heat, cover the pan and leave for at least 15 minutes. Remove the vanilla pod, scrape out all the seeds and stir them into the milk. Discard the pod.

3. Meanwhile, butter a smooth-sided 25½cm-diameter round glass or porcelain baking dish and use a large knife to slice off the top and bottom of the pineapple as well as the prickly rind. Go over the pineapple with a small knife nicking out the hairy 'eyes'.

Halve the pineapple lengthways and halve each half lengthways. Slice the quarters into 1cm triangles. Some pineapples need their central core removed because it's woody; if necessary, do this before you slice.

4. Lay out the wedges in the buttered dish and bake for 5 minutes. This pre-baking means the juices are reabsorbed into the pineapple and don't seep into the custard.

5. Meanwhile, whisk together the eggs, egg yolks, sugar, flour and crème fraîche or cream, and when amalgamated gradually whisk in the warm speckled milk.

6. Pour the custard mixture over the pineapple wedges. Bake for about 40 minutes until the custard is set and there are scorch marks where some of the pineapple has poked through.

Allow to cool for a few minutes (it will flop back into the dish) and serve dusted with icing sugar.

Gooseberry and Elderflower Tart with Frangipane Custard

Serves 4−6   *Preparation: 20 minutes. Cooking: 40 minutes.*

400g gooseberries
3 tbsp caster sugar
2 tbsp elderflower cordial

For the pastry:
9 heaped tbsp plain flour
pinch salt
75g cold butter
1−2 tbsp cold water

For the custard:
100g whole blanched almonds
2 tbsp butter
50g caster sugar
2 eggs, beaten

A friend introduced me recently to elderflower cordial and I'm hooked. I like its subtle but powerful scented flavour, described by Jane Grigson as a muscat sweetness, so much, that when the flowers came into bloom I made my own from the abundance of fume-free elderflowers that grow along the towpath nearby.

Elderflowers, and elderflower cordial, have a particular affinity with gooseberries. A tablespoon of cordial added to stewed gooseberries (plus plenty of sugar) will give that haunting muscat flavour. Lightly crushed and folded into thick cream or Greek yoghurt or a mixture of the two, it will make an excellent fool.

A spoonful or two of elderflower cordial is also an excellent thing to add to a gooseberry tart – and that's what I've done for this super-deluxe version. I blind-baked a shortcrust-pastry lining, filled it with gooseberries marinated in elderflower cordial and poured over an almond custard which I made in a trice in the food processor.

The custard puffs as it sets into a golden-crusted pillow dotted with the whole goosegogs poking through. Serve it with crème fraîche – its slightly lemony flavour goes particularly well – and caster sugar.

1. Top and tail the gooseberries, rinse under cold running water, drain and tip into a bowl. Sprinkle over 3 tablespoons of sugar and the elderflower cordial and stir well for a couple of minutes.

2. Pre-heat the oven to 350F/180C/gas mark 4.

3. To make the pastry: sift the flour and salt into a large mixing bowl. Cut the butter into small pieces and use your fingers to rub it quickly into the flour until it resembles heavy breadcrumbs. Add the water, a little at a time, until, using a knife or fork, you can stir it up into a clump. Flour a work surface and roll the pastry until you can cut a circle to fit a 20cm flan tin or a 25½cm tart tin. Oil the tin thoroughly and tuck the pastry into position, using scraps to plug any tears or cracks. Trim the top, cover loosely with a sheet of foil and half fill with rice or dried beans. Cook for 15 minutes. Remove the foil and pop back into the oven for 5 minutes. Remove from the oven.

4. Give the gooseberries another good stir.

5. Make the custard by processing the almonds into dust. With the motor running add the sugar, then butter, and finally the eggs, continuing just until the mixture is nicely amalgamated.

6. Tip the gooseberries and their juice into the pastry shell, smoothing them evenly, pour over the custard and return to the oven for a further 30 minutes or until the top is tawny and the gooseberries tender. Run a knife around the inside edge of the dish. Cover it with a large plate and invert the tart. Repeat with a second plate. Eat hot, warm or cold. Excellent for a picnic.

Mrs Langan's Chocolate Pudding

Serves 6　　　　　*Preparation: 25 minutes. Cooking: 15 minutes*

6 large eggs
75g caster sugar
50g cocoa
225ml double cream

For the chocolate sauce:
150g Green and Black's, Lindt
　　or Menier dark chocolate
50g unsalted butter
1 tsp water
icing sugar

Dark, bitter and black is how I like chocolate. For cooking it really is worth seeking out the very best quality chocolate. It's the cocoa-solid content that's the important ingredient. This gives chocolate its rich, powerful flavour and it's interesting that this finer, darker, more expensive stuff has a lower sugar and fat content than cheaper brands.

I can go for months without chocolate, but I keep a stash of Green and Black's dark chocolate (made with 70 per cent cocoa solids) for my occasional binges. It can be used to great effect in the chocolate sauce for my version of Mrs Langan's Chocolate Pudding. This was devised by the late, great restaurateur and named after his mother. It's been on the menu of Odin's since it opened twenty-one years ago.

The ingredients are curious – it has no fat or flour – but the result is a moist, springy sponge which is both light and substantial. It's actually a clever, foolproof recipe which is quick and easy and never fails to impress. It's also a cholesterol blow-out not suitable for dieters. Serve it as a post-Lenten treat.

1. Pre-heat the oven to 350F/180C/gas mark 4. Have ready a 30 ×17–20cm, 2½cm-deep baking tray lined with greaseproof paper.

2. Separate the eggs into two large mixing bowls. Whisk the yolks until thick. Still whisking, gradually add the sugar. When thick and thoroughly amalgamated, sift over the cocoa, whisking until nicely mixed.

3. Whisk the egg whites into soft peaks. Loosen up the chocolate mixture with a couple of spoonfuls of egg whites then slowly and gently cut and fold in the rest. Pour into the prepared tray and bake in the middle of the oven for 15 minutes exactly. Remove from the oven and leave to cool in the tin.

4. While the cake cools – it will settle back down into the tin – make the chocolate sauce. Break the chocolate into squares. Place in a small plastic bowl with the butter. Rest the bowl over a pan of gently boiling water and stir as the two ingredients melt and coagulate. Finally, stir in the water.

5. Whip the cream softly.

6. Dust the top of the cake with icing sugar, cover with transparent film and invert the cake. Spread with the chocolate sauce, leaving a 1¼cm border. Cover with the cream. Using the transparent film to help you, roll up the cake to make a stubby log. It's almost certain to crack as you roll but that's part of its charm. Slip on to a plate and dust again with more icing sugar.

For best results slice with a thin, sharp knife, wiping between slices. Excellent with strawberries or poached, stoned cherries.

Orange-Baked Semolina Pudding with Rhubarb

Serves 4   *Preparation: 15 minutes. Cooking: 35 minutes*

2 medium oranges
750ml milk
1 vanilla pod
4 tbsp demerara sugar
50g semolina
pinch salt

2 large eggs
freshly grated nutmeg
knob of butter
500g rhubarb
caster sugar to serve

What all traditional milky British puds share is the ability to be quite dreadful. Semolina is possibly the worst, yet when it is made with care – the milk well seasoned and a couple of eggs added – it is sublime.

I've divided the cooking into three stages for this creamy, soufflé-like pudding with a pleasingly crusted surface.

To go along with it – and cooking at the same time in the oven – I made a dish of rhubarb, flavoured with orange zest. Instead of water, I squeezed fresh orange juice over chunks of particularly beautiful pinky-red rhubarb with a little sugar. The dish is covered with foil and the fruit becomes tender without losing its form.

Both semolina and rhubarb are delicious on their own, but combine together in one of those culinary marriages made in heaven, especially when eaten with a dusting of extra sugar (unrefined demerara in the cooking and caster sugar later) and a dollop of something rich and creamy such as Greek yoghurt, thick cream or crème fraîche.

Like all milk puddings, this is best served warm.

1. Use a potato peeler to remove the zest from one orange. Place four strips in a saucepan with 600ml of the milk and the vanilla pod. Bring slowly to the boil, allowing about 10 minutes for this, giving the vanilla pod a good bash to release its tiny black seeds. Remove from the heat, stir in 2 tablespoons of the demerara, cover the pan and set aside.

2. Meanwhile, place the remaining milk, semolina and pinch of salt in a small pan. Place over a low flame and stir constantly while it thickens, which it will quickly do. Remove from the heat and allow to cool slightly.

3. Separate the eggs and use a wooden spoon to stir the yolks into the semolina, thus slackening the mixture. Season generously with nutmeg.

4. Pour the flavoured milk through a sieve into the mixture, first a cupful which you stir until smooth, and then the rest. You shouldn't have any lumps but if you do, give the mixture a good beating with a wire whisk.

5. Then whisk the egg whites into firm peaks and fold into the mixture. Pour into a buttered earthenware or ceramic gratin dish.

6. Cut the rhubarb into chunks, discarding any root and silky strands. Rinse and lay out in another gratin dish. Tuck the remaining orange zest between the layers, squeeze over the juice of the oranges and sprinkle the remaining demerara over. Cover with foil.

7. Turn the oven to 325F/170C/gas mark 3, place the rhubarb near the bottom, and when the temperature comes up put the pudding on a middle shelf. Cook for 30 minutes or until the pudding has a golden surface and is just set, and the rhubarb tender.

Plum (or Cherry) Clafoutis

Serves 6   *Preparation: 20 minutes.*
                          Cooking: 30 minutes (plus 30 minutes optional resting)

10 large or 18 smaller ripe red
    dessert plums or 500g
    Rainier cherries
1 knob butter
4 eggs

100g caster sugar
50g flour
300ml single cream, or half
    cream and half milk, or all
    milk

Clafoutis is one of the most seductive puddings. It's made with a sugary thick batter mixture which is poured over plump and slightly tart fruit – traditionally cherries – and it billows beautifully, with the fruit poking through like traffic lights.

It's not dissimilar to a soufflé, but is cooked in a shallow dish, and there's almost no chance of its going wrong. And timing is not something you have to worry about.

In fact, although it looks beautifully bouffant when it comes out of the oven and it's tempting to serve it immediately, clafoutis is better left in the dying heat of the oven to rest and settle back on itself.

It might not look as dramatic after 30 minutes, but that's the best time to eat it, when the sweet and slightly bouncy soft egg is in perfect contrast to the sourness of the gently weeping fruit.

In early August, when the last of the super-duper American cherries need eating up and European cherries are coming on line, is the perfect time for a cherry clafoutis.

It's also a good time to make a plum version. The plums work best if they are halved through their circumference and the stones removed. The cherry version is best made with the stones left intact as they contribute to the flavour (and are a bore to remove).

The batter is at its richest and softest made with single cream, but will be almost as good with half and half (cream and milk) or all milk. Serve the clafoutis with caster sugar and a bowl of thick cream.

1. Pre-heat the oven to 350F/180C/gas mark 4. Use the butter to grease generously a 23 ×30cm gratin-type ceramic dish.

2. Rinse the plums and halve through their circumference. If they're not entirely ripe you might need to do a bit of work with a small sharp knife, scraping down the stone to loosen it from the flesh. Lay the plum halves, cut side up, in the dish. If making cherry clafoutis, remove the cherry stalks and rinse the cherries. Lay them out in the buttered dish.

3. Make the mixture by whisking the eggs in a large bowl, then stir in the sugar. When it's completely amalgamated, sieve over the flour, a little at a time. Carry on whisking or beating with a wooden spoon until the mixture is smooth. Now add the cream, or cream and milk, or milk, whisking or beating merely until it's mixed. Pour the batter over the plums or cherries. Bake the clafoutis in the pre-heated oven for 30 minutes or until the egg mixture has set and the plums or cherries are tender and weeping slightly. Turn off the oven and leave the clafoutis for up to 30 minutes before serving. It is, however, quite wonderful cold and is one of the finest breakfasts I know. But it rarely hangs around that long.

Peach Sandwiches with Almond Cream

Serves 6   *Preparation: 30 minutes. Cooking: 15 minutes*

6 tender peaches
icing sugar
250g ready-made puff pastry

For the syrup:
600ml water
100g caster sugar
1 orange
squeeze of lemon

½ cinnamon stick
1 vanilla pod

For the cream:
6 tbsp thick cream
25g ground almonds
2 tsp peach liqueur
2 tsp poaching liquid

Have you noticed that peaches are gradually turning into nectarines? Most of them have lost their fluff and the skin seems thinner and to have turned several shades darker.

Peaches seem to have taken over from strawberries as *the* glut fruit of the summer, and prices seem surprisingly low. Best of all are the huge white-flesh peaches which are heady with scent and a sumptuous treat to eat raw.

Buying peaches and nectarines that require 'ripening', as is almost always the case when you go for those bargain punnets, involves risk. Both these fruit ripen on the tree and all you can hope for is that they will soften before any bruises turn mouldy. Invariably you end up with a bowl of crinkly bottoms which all turn 'ripe' at the same moment. This, then, is the time to make a peach or nectarine tart, or to poach them gently as I've done in this recipe.

It involves sugary discs of puff pastry which aren't allowed to puff and which sandwich poached peaches and cream. The cream is flavoured with some of the poaching liquid, a dash of peach liqueur and ground almonds. It's actually very simple to make and can all be done in advance but needs quick, last-minute assembly. These pastry discs are an idea nicked from Marco Pierre White; don't worry if they don't look immaculate, as his always do – imperfections can be disguised with icing sugar.

1. If the peach skin won't peel away, pour boiling water over the peaches, drain after 15 seconds and peel. Put the skin in a pan that can hold the peaches in a single layer with the water, sugar, cinnamon, vanilla and lemon juice. Use a potato peeler to pare the orange zest (no white pith) and add it and the orange juice to the pan. Bring slowly to the boil, stirring as the sugar dissolves, and leave to simmer gently for a couple of minutes. Add the peaches, cover and cook gently, turning half-way through, for 10 minutes. Remove the peaches to cool, then cut into quarters or chunks. Reserve the poaching liquid.

2. Pre-heat the oven to 400F/200C/gas mark 6. Dust a work surface with icing sugar and roll out the pastry to make a 23 × 35cm slab. Tightly roll it up like a swiss roll. Slice into 12 pieces and, using more icing sugar, roll out until paper-thin. Place on a non-stick baking sheet and cook for around 10 minutes until golden. Flip the discs over on to a work surface and bang flat with the base of a saucepan. Return to the oven for 5–10 minutes, bash again and then slip on to a wire rack to cool and harden. Make the cream by mixing everything together.

3. When you're ready to eat, place a dollop of cream in the centre of each plate. Cover with a disc, more cream and a share of peaches, more cream and a disc. Spoon poaching juices around the sandwich and dust with icing sugar. Wait for the ooh ahs.

Prune and Almond Frittata with Crème Fraîche

Serves 4–6   *Preparation: 20 minutes. Cooking: 20 minutes*

150g pre-cooked stoned
   prunes
1 mug of black tea
2 tbsp brandy (optional)
2 tbsp flaked almonds
splash cooking oil

6 fresh eggs
4 tbsp ground almonds
2 flat tbsp caster sugar
50g butter
2 tbsp icing sugar (approx.)
crème fraîche

Half a dozen eggs, a few prunes and some almonds, a cup of black tea and a little sugar, and you have the makings of a quick and spectacular pudding that will more than satisfy four hungry guests.

I was tempted to make this dish while reading Paul Gaylor's smashing book, *Great Value Gourmet* (Weidenfeld and Nicolson).

There are many excellent ideas here: French onion soup with herring crostini, Thai chicken wings in spiced coconut milk, fettucine with charred tomatoes and rosemary oil, daube of rabbit with orange, cinnamon and rosemary – with half the recipes illustrated by 'eat me' photos.

But back to the frittata. This is the Italian version of a Spanish omelette. It's always made to share and is a thick, stuffed omelette to eat hot, warm or cold, served in big wedges like a cake. Cooked badly it will be dry, rubbery and dull, no matter how distinguished the filling. Carefully cooked, it has a texture as soft and springy as a soufflé, providing a delicious eggy background for the filling.

Unlike a rolled omelette, which is cooked very quickly in the minimum amount of butter, a frittata takes about 15 minutes over a low flame – the idea being to let the eggs set without scorching the bottom – and it needs plenty of butter that will bubble up gently at the sides of the pan.

A heavy-bottomed frying pan is best for cooking this type of omelette and I'd also recommend using a heat diffuser. The last bit of cooking is done very quickly under a pre-heated grill when the heat also caramelizes a dusting of icing sugar.

1. Halve the prunes, place in a small saucepan with the tea and simmer until almost evaporated. This takes about 6 minutes. Then pour the brandy (if used) over the prunes and cook until it turns to a sticky juice.
2. Meanwhile, heat the cooking oil in a frying pan over a low medium heat and 'toast' the flaked almonds, tossing them around as they brown. Drain on kitchen paper. Wipe out the frying pan.
3. Beat the eggs in a mixing bowl and stir in the ground almonds and sugar. Heat the clean frying pan over a medium–low flame, add the butter and, when bubbling, add the egg mixture. Turn down the heat immediately and spread the prunes and their juices over the egg. Leave to cook very, very slowly for about 15 minutes until the omelette is firm and set but the top is still very slightly liquid. At this point pre-heat the grill.
4. Sprinkle over the flaked almonds and dust (through a sieve or tea strainer) with half the icing sugar. Hold the pan up close to the grill for a few seconds while the sugar melts and crystallizes.
5. Let the omelette settle in the pan for a minute or so and then gently ease it away from the sides with a palette knife and work the knife under the omelette – it should come away easily.
6. Slip on to a plate, dust with the remaining sugar and eat immediately with plenty of crème fraîche.

Strawberry Tart with Mascarpone and Balsamic Vinegar

Serves 6–8   *Preparation: 20 minutes. Cooking: 15 minutes*

1 tbsp butter, lard or oil

225g ready-made shortcrust
  pastry

flour

700g strawberries

250g tub mascarpone

400g thick Greek yoghurt

1 tbsp balsamic vinegar

2 tbsp caster sugar

4 tbsp redcurrant jelly

1 tbsp water

In early June we are usually enjoying an overabundance of strawberries as the first home-grown crop arrives in the shops, but not always. If we aren't, it will be the weather that's to blame because supermarkets have been busily trying to extend the season because we can't get enough of strawberries, and British are best. They plant them under glass, then move on to poly tunnels, and finally, when skies the length and breadth of the country are supposed to be sunny, they move outdoors for the main crop.

The first English crops on sale have generally been raised under glass, and, judging by my sample of Elsanta (from M&S), there's little wrong with the flavour. Prices, however, can be sky-high, with better buys available from France, Spain and the States.

I've broken away from the usual combination of strawberries and cream for this recipe and used a mixture of mascarpone and thick yoghurt whipped together with a splash of balsamic vinegar. The vinegar, with its simultaneously sweet and spicy flavour, gives the cream a surprising richness which offsets the natural sweetness of the strawberries beautifully.

For the sake of convenience I've used ready-made pastry; the case could be made twenty-four hours in advance but the topping should be added no more than an hour before, otherwise the pastry begins to turn soggy. If you prefer, these ingredients can be used to make eight individual tartlets.

1. Pre-heat the oven to 400F/200C/gas mark 6.

2. Oil a 25½cm metal tart dish or 8 ×10cm tartlet tins.

3. Dust a work surface with flour and roll out the pastry quite thinly (about 3mm). Roll the pastry loosely around the rolling pin and drape it over the tart tin(s). Roll the rolling pin over the top to remove any excess pastry and gently press the pastry into the tin(s) and up the sides. Set the tin(s) on a baking sheet and prick the dough with a fork. Chill until the oven comes up to temperature.

4. Line the tart(s) with foil and half-fill with rice or dried beans. Cook for 8 minutes, remove the foil and its contents and cook for 5 more minutes until the pastry is cooked but not scorched. Remove the pastry case(s) and leave to cool on a wire rack. Place on a serving plate.

5. Rinse the strawberries quickly under cold running water, drain and remove the stems (which act as a plug and stop them absorbing the water).

6. In a large bowl, mix together the mascarpone and yoghurt, and beat in the balsamic vinegar. Gently smear the cream evenly into the pastry case(s) then cover with upright strawberries all neatly lined up.

7. Heat through the redcurrant jelly, stirring in the water to thin it slightly. Sprinkle the strawberries lightly with sugar and then, using a pastry brush, carefully paint them with the jelly (the sugar helps it to stick to the berries). Serve immediately.

Tarte Tatin/Upside-Down Apple Tart

Serves 4   *Preparation: 30 minutes. Cooking: 30 minutes*

50g butter
4 heaped tbsp caster sugar
   (approx. 100g)
generous squeeze lemon juice

8 small Cox's apples
175g (half a packet)
   ready-made puff pastry
crème fraîche

On holiday in Brittany one summer I was taken to lunch at a St Malo restaurant which specializes in Tarte Tatin. At À La Duchesse Anne, there is no chance of being offered a dried-up slice of this famous French upside-down apple tart. There it's always made to order to be eaten hot from the oven.

It's an impressively unusual-looking tart made by cooking butter and sugar together, and when the mixture caramelizes, planting peeled quarter apples in the toffee and tucking it up with pastry. When it emerges from the oven, the pan is inverted and hey presto! Those apples now appear to have turned into giant conkers set in a glistening, glossy, golden mould. It's the distinctive burnt flavour that's so addictive and it goes particularly well with the slight sharpness of crème fraîche. Back home, after much trial and error, and with the help of Jane Grigson's version of the original 1900 recipe (from her little-known *Food With The Famous*, Grub Street), I now knock out Tarte Tatin all the time. It's really very easy.

1. Pre-heat the oven to 400F/200C/gas mark 6 and place an oven sheet on a shelf near the top.

2. Over a moderate heat, melt the butter in a 24 ×4cm sturdy metal flat tin, frying pan or similar. Sprinkle on the sugar and keep stirring as it melts, froths and gradually turns through shades of amber to dark brown. In my first efforts I was wary of letting it go too dark and ending up with a bitter caramel, but the colour and thus intensity of the burnt flavour are a matter of taste you'll only discover by trial and error. If the sugar turns to crystals, which it sometimes does, don't worry, this is the time to add the lemon juice. If the mixture appears not to want to crystallize, keep going. It will eventually. When you're satisfied, remove the pan from the heat.

3. Quarter, core and peel the apples. Plant them rounded side down in the toffee (don't worry if it turns hard), fitting them snugly into one layer.

4. Roll out the pastry and cut a circle to fit inside the tin. Press it lightly over the apples, tucking it down the sides.

5. As soon as the oven is ready, place the tin on the oven tray and cook for 30 minutes until the pastry is puffed and golden. Remove from the oven and run a knife round the inside edge of the tin. Cover the tart with a large plate and quickly invert the tin, taking care for the inevitable juices. Divide into four and eat with plenty of crème fraîche.

Index